1989

AGEING POPULATIONS

THE SOCIAL POLICY IMPLICATIONS

ORGANISATION FOR ECONOMIC CO-OPERATION AND DEVELOPMENT

Publié en français sous le titre :

LE VIEILLISSEMENT DÉMOGRAPHIQUE :
CONSÉQUENCES POUR LA POLITIQUE SOCIALE

Across the OECD area, demographic change during the 20th century has been characterised by important secular trends towards low fertility and increasing life expectancy, interrupted by one cycle during which fertility rates first rose then sharply declined. *Demographic Change and Public Policy* is a new publication series which is being introduced by the OECD at a time when the implications of these demographic changes are increasingly being taken into account in the formulation of public policy in all OECD countries.

Since the mid-1960s in particular, all OECD countries have experienced a major decline in fertility rates to levels which are now, with the exception of Ireland and Turkey, significantly below the level required to replace the population. As a direct result, almost all OECD countries face an increasingly older population structure – a trend which is expected to be reinforced by a further decline in mortality. The proportion of people aged over 65 in the population will increase, gradually at first, then more rapidly after the turn of the century until by the year 2040 the proportion of people over 65 will, on average, have risen to almost double its present level.

In addition to the impact of changing fertility and mortality rates, the population of OECD countries has been influenced by migration flows, with some countries experiencing significant levels of emigration and others receiving large inflows of migrants. These flows have had an important effect in the past, not only on the size of populations, but also on their structure, and will continue to influence future developments through their effect on subsequent generations.

Alongside, and associated with changes in the age structure and numerical size of populations, there have occurred profound changes in family size, household structure and social attitudes towards formal and informal relationships between men, women and their families. These demographic changes are already affecting the general economy, the labour market, and a range of social policies related to education, health care, pension provision, family and child support, and migration, and they will continue to have an important impact in the future. Because of the long lead times involved in adapting policy in many of these areas, an effort must be made, as far as possible, to anticipate future demographic developments and to co-ordinate policy responses in the social, labour market and economic spheres. It is the objective of this new publication series to address the wide range of public policy issues arising from demographic changes.

This first volume, which is based on work undertaken by OECD's Manpower and Social Affairs Committee and its Working Party on Social Policy, focuses on the implications of ageing population structures for social policy. The study, prepared by Maria Maguire of the Directorate for Social Affairs, Manpower and Education, considers the issues within a quantitative framework. It examines past and future demographic trends in OECD countries, analyses the impact of these trends on projected demographic dependency ratios and social expenditure, and discusses the policy options available to respond to the demographic pressures expected early next century. The study is published on the responsibility of the Secretary-General.

Other volumes planned for the series will consider the economic and social consequences of current demographic developments, the demographic aspects of migration, and the impact of demographic changes on the labour market.

James R. Gass
Director, Social Affairs,
Manpower and Education

Also available

«OECD: Social Policy Studies» Series

No. 5   REFORMING PUBLIC PENSIONS (July 1988)

No. 4   FINANCING AND DELIVERING HEALTH CARE. A Comparative Analysis of OECD Countries (July 1987)
(81 87 02 1) ISBN 92-64-12973-1   102 pages   £6.00   US$13.00   F60.00   DM26.00

No. 3   LIVING CONDITIONS IN OECD COUNTRIES. A Compendium of Social Indicators (February 1986)
(81 85 04 1) ISBN 92-64-12734-8   166 pages   £6.50   US$13.00   F65.00   DM29.00

No. 2   MEASURING HEALTH CARE 1950-1983. Expenditure, Costs and Performance (November 1985)
(81 85 06 1) ISBN 92-64-12736-4   162 pages   £9.00   US$18.00   F90.00   DM40.00

No. 1   SOCIAL EXPENDITURE 1960-1990. Problems of Growth and Control (March 1985)
(81 85 01 1) ISBN 92-64-12656-2   98 pages   £7.50   US$15.00   F75.00   DM33.00

STRUCTURAL ADJUSTMENT AND ECONOMIC PERFORMANCE (February 1988)
(03 87 02 1) ISBN 92-64-13006-3   372 pages   £19.50   US$39.95   F195.00   DM84.00

OECD EMPLOYMENT OUTLOOK. SEPTEMBER 1987 (October 1987)
(81 87 03 1) ISBN 92-64-13007-1   220 pages   £16.00   US$34.00   F160.00   DM69.00

EMPLOYMENT GROWTH AND STRUCTURAL CHANGE (February 1985)
(81 85 02 1) ISBN 92-64-12659-7   226 pages   £9.50   US$19.00   F95.00   DM42.00

Prices charged at the OECD Bookshop.

*THE OECD CATALOGUE OF PUBLICATIONS and supplements will be sent free of charge
on request addressed either to OECD Publications Service,
2, rue André-Pascal, 75775 PARIS CEDEX 16, or to the OECD Distributor in your country.*

TABLE OF CONTENTS

Foreword 7

Part I

DEMOGRAPHIC TRENDS AND POPULATION AGEING

Chapter 1

POPULATION TRENDS IN HISTORICAL
   PERSPECTIVE 11

Causes of Population Ageing 12
Demographic Trends in the Post-war Period 12

Chapter 2

PROJECTED DEMOGRAPHIC TRENDS TO
   2050 16
Reliability of Demographic Projections 16

Projections of Fertility, Mortality and Migration
   Rates 17
Projected Trends in the Growth Rate and Age
   Structure of Populations 18
Trends in the Elderly Population 20
Trends in the Working-age Population 24
Trends in the Young Population 25

Notes and references 26
Summary of Part I 26

Part II

THE IMPLICATIONS OF AGEING POPULATIONS FOR SOCIAL EXPENDITURE

Chapter 3

TRENDS IN DEMOGRAPHIC DEPENDENCY
   RATIOS 29

Chapter 4

POPULATION AGEING AND SOCIAL
   EXPENDITURE 33

The Distribution of Social Expenditure by Age
   Groups 33
Methodology for Projecting the Impact of
   Demographic Factors on Social Expenditure 35
Projected Trends in Social Expenditure 35

The Capacity to Finance Social Expenditure
   Increases 39

Chapter 5

SENSITIVITY OF EXPENDITURE
   PROJECTIONS TO UNDERLYING
   ASSUMPTIONS 43

Demographic Assumptions 43
Economic Assumptions 44
Assumptions Concerning Real Benefit Levels 46

Notes and references 46
Summary of Part II 47

Part III

POLICY ISSUES AND CHOICES

Chapter 6

RESTRUCTURING SOCIAL EXPENDITURE . . 51

Family Benefits 51
Health Care 51
Education 52

Chapter 7

THE IMPACT OF POPULATION AGEING ON
   PRODUCTIVITY AND THE LABOUR FORCE 54

Population Ageing and Productivity 54

Labour Force Prospects 55
Migrant Workers 58
Prospects for Labour Supply of Youth and Women . 58
Labour Supply of Older Workers 58

Chapter 8

ISSUES IN HEALTH CARE POLICY 62

Past Growth of Public Health Care Expenditure . . . 62
Prospects for Health Care Expenditure in the Future 62
Policy Issues 66

Chapter 9

ISSUES IN PENSION POLICY   69

Past Growth of Public Pension Expenditure   69
Sources of Future Expenditure Growth   69
Policy Issues   70

Notes and references   73
Summary of Part III   74
Annex A: DEMOGRAPHIC PROJECTIONS . . .   77
Annex B: SOCIAL EXPENDITURE
PROJECTIONS   85

FOREWORD

Important changes are projected in the demographic structure of OECD countries over the next half-century. Low fertility and mortality rates are combining to reduce the rate of population growth and produce a substantial increase in the proportion of elderly people, thereby causing ageing of the population structure. The proportion of elderly people has already increased considerably in many countries over the past several decades. Only a modest increase is projected in most countries between now and the early part of the next century, but shortly after the year 2000 the proportion of elderly people will begin to increase rapidly as the large numbers of people born during the so-called baby boom which followed World War II begin to reach the threshold of old age. This trend is reinforced by a decline in the proportion of young people in the population, resulting from low fertility rates. In the majority of OECD countries, fertility rates are now below the level required for replacement of the population. The proportion of the population in the working age groups is also expected to decline in most countries after the turn of the century.

This process of population ageing is common to almost all OECD countries, although there are considerable differences in its extent and timing. Most countries face a sharp increase in the proportion of elderly people from the early part of the next century, although for some the process is more gradual. In a minority of countries rapid population ageing is already occurring. The most striking example is Japan, where the proportion of the elderly is expected to increase by approximately two-thirds between 1980 and 2000.

Demographic projections are, of course, subject to considerable uncertainty, because both birth rates and mortality rates may change in unexpected ways. Nevertheless, the age structure can be predicted with a reasonable degree of certainty up to the turn of the century since the impact of birth rate changes up to this point will be relatively slight and mortality rates are likely to change relatively slowly. Beyond the turn of the century the projections become increasingly less certain, but barring very rapid changes in the underlying demographic variables, broad shifts in age structure can be foreseen. The sharp increase in the proportion of elderly people from the early part of the next century is predictable as a result mainly of the large population bulge caused by the post-war baby boom, which is gradually working its way through the age structure. Different assumptions about fertility and mortality trends affect the magnitude of the increase but they do not prevent it from happening.

Projected ageing of OECD populations raises concern about the implications for social expenditure and social policy, as well as the consequences for the labour market and the economy. This study focuses on the implications for social policy, although it also touches on some of the broader economic issues. Changes in age structure are likely to affect the demand for public social programmes, by increasing the demographic pressure on pension schemes, health care systems and other social services for the elderly, and reducing the demand for family benefits, education and other programmes catering to the young population. Two key concerns in this context are, first, the extent to which public social expenditure may have to be restructured to take account of changing demographic demands, and, second, the extent to which total outlays may rise as a result of demographic factors. Population ageing will also affect the size and structure of the labour force. The working age population is expected to shrink in most countries after the turn of the century and the proportion of middle aged and older workers will increase significantly. Such changes give rise to concerns over the possible effects on economic growth and possible difficulties in adapting the labour market to an ageing workforce. Changes in the size and structure of the working age population also have important implications for the capacity of society to finance social programmes. Since social programmes are financed largely from taxes and social security contributions paid by the working population, the prospect of a decline in the number of working age people, coupled with a significant increase in the proportion of elderly, has raised fears that the fiscal burden may increase steeply and that the financing of social programmes may be jeopardized.

Demographic changes will occur in the context of evolving economic and social institutions. The demands on social programmes will change as a result of non-demographic factors, and existing social policies will have on-going effects on the provision of benefits and services. Some of these factors may act to reduce demographic pressures, others will tend to magnify them. The labour market and the broader economy will also be affected by a range of non-demographic factors which will alter the capacity to finance social programmes over the coming decades. Moreover, it is likely that demographic changes themselves will trigger reactions in the economy and in social policy which will make it easier to cope with the effects of a changing age structure.

The first part of this study reviews recent demographic trends in OECD countries and sets out projected demographic changes up to the year 2050. Prospects for the growth and age structure of populations are outlined, with particular focus on trends in the numbers and proportion of elderly people, and trends affecting the working age population. One principal set of demographic projections has been made, and serves as the benchmark estimates for this study. Several variant projections have also been made in order to test the sensitivity of the benchmark projections to changes in fertility and mortality assumptions.

The second part deals with the implications of projected demographic changes for social expenditure and for the capacity to finance social programmes. The approach adopted here is to project expenditure on the basis of the existing age pattern of public social outlays, assuming that programme coverage and real per capita social benefits remain unchanged. This enables the impact of pure demographic change to be isolated from other factors which will influence the development of social expenditure. The expenditure projections are then compared with projections of the working age population which, assuming fixed labour force participation rates and unemployment, becomes a measure of the ability to support increased social outlays. It must be emphasized that the objective of this analysis is to produce projections, not predictions, of how demographic change will alter the level and stucture of social expenditure and the financing burden. Quite apart from the fact that population projections become increasingly less reliable as the projection period lengthens, the actual course of development will be influenced by policy responses to demographic pressures and by spontaneous reactions in social and economic institutions.

The final part of the study examines four key areas where adjustment is likely to be necessary in order to cope with the effects of demographic change. This part begins with a discussion of the changes in the structure of public social expenditure which are implied by demographic change. Such restructuring would reduce the growth of total social outlays caused by demographic change, but is likely to require considerable political and managerial skill. The second area examined is the labour market, with a focus on how shrinkage and ageing of the working age population may affect productivity and labour supply. The key issue addressed in this context is whether labour market trends are likely to ease or exacerbate the problem of financing social programmes, and what potential there may be for policy intervention to increase the size and productivity of the labour force. The final areas examined are health care and pensions, where policy developments are likely to have a significant impact on the development of expenditure and on the capacity to respond effectively to the needs of a growing elderly population. The implications of existing policies are examined, an assessment is made of the extent to which non-demographic factors, such as changes in real benefit levels, are likely to add to demographic pressures, and options for policy change are discussed.

Part I

DEMOGRAPHIC TRENDS AND POPULATION AGEING

INTRODUCTION

The ageing of the populations of OECD countries is largely a phenomenon of the twentieth century. Before 1900 only a very few countries experienced population ageing. The rate of ageing has varied considerably between countries, but the trend is apparent throughout the OECD area and current demographic projections by the OECD Secretariat indicate that it is likely to continue well into the twenty-first century.

Part I provides an overview of recent trends and sets out the main features of projected developments up to 2050. Although the discussion focuses primarily on general patterns of change, attention is also drawn to the most important cross-national variations. Historical data and projections for all countries are shown in Annex A.

The first chapter provides a historical perspective through a brief review of demographic developments since the last century and a more detailed exposition of trends in the period since the Second World War. The second chapter sets out projected developments up to 2050, based on population projections prepared by the OECD Secretariat. Following a discussion of the assumptions about future changes in fertility, mortality and international migration (the three basic determinants of population change), prospects for the overall growth and age structure of populations are examined. This is followed by a more detailed analysis of the extent and timing of projected changes in the proportion of elderly persons, in their numbers and in the age and sex structure of the elderly population. The implications of demographic change for the growth and age structure of the working age population are also analysed. Part I concludes with a brief look at projected trends in the young population.

Chapter 1

POPULATION TRENDS IN HISTORICAL PERSPECTIVE

For the purposes of consistency in demographic analysis it is usual to designate fixed ages as the boundaries of youth, working age and old age, although in practice the ages used to define these population groups tend to vary across countries and from one context to another. In this study the young population is defined as those under age 15, the working age population as those between the ages of 15 and 64 and the elderly population as those aged 65 and over.

At the beginning of this century the countries which are now OECD Members had very small elderly populations. People aged 65 and over typically accounted for between 4 and 6 per cent of the population, although in France and Sweden, where the ageing trend began in the nineteenth century, the proportion of elderly was over 8 per cent[1]. The majority of OECD countries have experienced substantial ageing of their populations since the beginning of this century, although the rate has varied considerably (see Chart 1). At the turn of the century, for example, Canada and Germany had similar proportions of elderly people, but by 1980 the proportion in Germany had more than trebled whereas the proportion in Canada had increased less than twice. The Japanese population did not begin to age until the 1940s but the proportion of elderly almost doubled between 1940 and 1980.

In the period 1950 to 1980, the average proportion aged 65 and over in the OECD area rose by over 40 per cent to reach 12.2 per cent (Table 1). The ageing trend has been most pronounced in the countries of Northern and Western Europe, where, with a few exceptions, the proportion of elderly people exceeds 13.5 per cent of the total population; in Austria and Germany the proportion exceeds 15 per cent, and in Sweden it is over 16 per cent. The Southern European countries generally have between 10 and 13 per cent of their populations in the elderly age group, and Finland, Iceland, Ireland and the Netherlands also fall within this range. Of the non-European countries, the United States, with over 11 per cent of the population aged 65 and over, currently has the highest proportion of elderly. In the other non-European countries the proportion is still relatively low, ranging between 9 and 10 per cent. Turkey does not conform to the general trend described here since its population has only begun to age comparatively recently and the proportion of elderly people is still at the level

Chart 1

PROPORTIONS OF PERSONS AGED 65 AND OVER IN TOTAL POPULATION 1850-1980

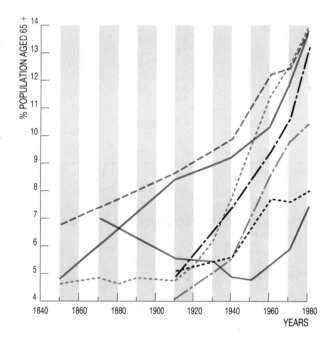

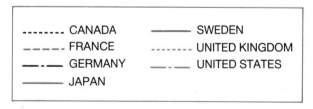

Sources:

John F. Ermisch, *The Political Economy of Demographic Change,* London, Heinemann, 1983, Table 1.7; Government of Japan, *The Population of Japan: Trends and Implications,* paper presented at International Conference on Population, Mexico City, 6-13th August 1984, Table 1; Peter Laslett, 'Societal Development and Ageing' in Robert H. Binstock and Ethel Shanas eds., *Handbook of Ageing and the Social Sciences* (second edition), New York, Van Nostrand Reinhold Company 1985, pp. 199-230, Table 4.

Table 1. **Percentage of population aged 65 and over, 1950-1980**

	1950	1960	1970	1980
Canada	7.7	7.6	8.0	9.5
France	11.4	11.6	12.9	14.0
Germany	9.4	10.6	13.2	15.5
Italy	8.0	9.1	10.9	13.5
Japan	5.2	5.7	7.1	9.1
United Kingdom	10.7	11.7	13.0	14.9
United States	8.1	9.2	9.8	11.3
Average of above[a]	8.6	9.4	10.7	12.5
Australia	8.1	8.5	8.3	9.6
Austria	10.4	11.9	14.1	15.5
Belgium	11.0	12.0	13.4	14.4
Denmark	9.1	10.6	12.3	14.4
Finland	6.7	7.5	9.2	12.0
Greece	6.8	8.1	11.1	13.1
Iceland	7.6	8.1	8.8	9.9
Ireland	10.7	11.1	10.8	10.7
Luxembourg	9.8	10.8	12.4	13.5
Netherlands	7.7	8.6	10.2	11.5
New Zealand	9.0	8.7	8.5	9.7
Norway	9.6	11.1	12.9	14.8
Portugal	7.0	8.0	9.3	10.2
Spain	7.3	8.2	9.6	10.9
Sweden	10.3	11.8	13.7	16.3
Switzerland	9.6	11.0	11.7	13.8
Turkey	3.4	3.7	4.4	4.7
OECD average[a]	8.5	9.4	10.6	12.2

a) Unweighted average.
Source: Annex A, Table A.2.

reached in most other OECD countries at the beginning of this century.

Causes of Population Ageing

Changes in the age structure of a population are determined by trends in fertility, mortality and international migration. The importance of each of these factors has varied over time and across countries, but the ageing of OECD populations has been caused primarily by a long-term decline in fertility.

Over the past two centuries industrialised countries have undergone a demographic transition characterised by a move from high to low levels of both fertility and mortality, although the exact timing and pattern of change have varied between countries. However, whereas mortality has declined more or less continuously since the nineteenth century, the decline in fertility was, in most cases, interrupted by a major upturn in birth rates in the two decades following the World War II.

Most Western countries experienced a phase of mortality decline and rapid population growth during the first three quarters of the nineteenth century. In Japan this phase occurred between the late nineteenth century and World War II, and in Turkey it was later

still. Fertility rates began declining in Western countries in the last quarter of the nineteenth century and continued to fall up to the eve of the Second World War. Mortality rates also continued to decline, but as the fall in fertility was more rapid, population growth rates slowed. By the late 1930s fertility rates in a number of countries were below the level required for replacement of the population and population growth was negligible.

The substantial increase in the proportion of elderly people in Western countries, which occurred from around the turn of this century, was due primarily to the long-term downward trend in fertility, which reduced the number of births and led to a decline in the proportion of young people. The decline in mortality did not have a major effect on the age structure of populations since it affected all age groups. In fact, mortality decreased more at young ages than older ones, thereby offsetting rather than exacerbating the effect of fertility changes. Between 1900 and 1950 life expectancy at birth in western countries increased, on average, by almost 20 years for females and by over 18 years for males. In the same period life expectancy at age 65 rose by 2.5 years for females and by less than two years for males[2].

International migration was an important source of population change in a number of western countries in the nineteenth and early twentieth centuries. There were large outflows of emigrants from Europe to North America, Australia and New Zealand, as well as migration between some Europeam countries. International migration decreased considerably after the First World War and, apart from movement of political refugees in the inter-war period and after World War II, it has, with a few exceptions, been a relatively minor element in population change since then.

Although a number of Western countries appeared to be approaching a phase of zero population growth in the late 1930s, characterised by a stabilisation of fertility and mortality in equilibrium at low levels, the period since the early 1940s has seen a significant departure from the predicted trend. While mortality rates have continued to decline, there was a major and generalised upturn in fertility rates, the so-called baby boom, which lasted from the middle of World War II up to the mid-1960s. This development reversed the decline in population growth rates and reduced the rate of population ageing. Subsequently the decline in fertility resumed, although there have been some signs of a levelling-off in the trend in recent years.

Demographic Trends in the Post-war Period

Chart 2 illustrates how fertility rates have changed in the period since 1940. The fertility measure used here is the total fertility rate, which is the sum of age-specific fertility rates over all ages of the child-bearing period. This gives an indication of the number of children an

Chart 2

TOTAL FERTILITY RATES
1940-1983

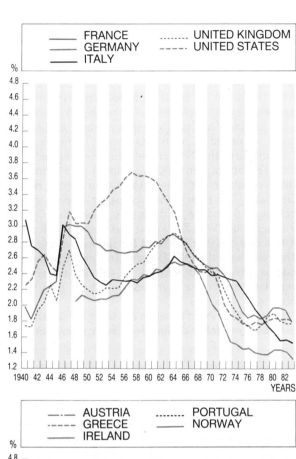

FRANCE
GERMANY
ITALY
UNITED KINGDOM
UNITED STATES

DENMARK
SWEDEN
NETHERLANDS
BELGIUM
FINLAND

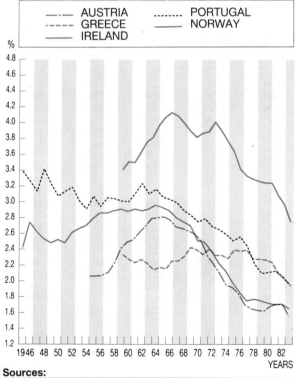

AUSTRIA
GREECE
IRELAND
PORTUGAL
NORWAY

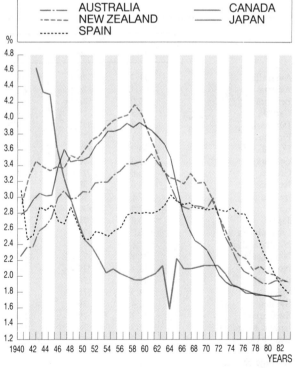

AUSTRALIA
NEW ZEALAND
SPAIN
CANADA
JAPAN

Sources:

Patrick Festy, *La Fécondité des pays occidentaux de 1870 à 1970,* Paris, Presses universitaires de France, 1979; Report on Past and Projected Movements in Fertility in OECD Countries prepared for OECD by Michael J. Murphy, London School of Economics, 1985 (mimeo); Data for the United States provided by *United States Bureau of the Census.*

average woman would have if she experienced the current age-specific fertility rates over her reproductive years.

The most striking features of the trends shown in Chart 2 are the proximity of the major turning points in fertility in the various countries, and the convergence of fertility rates over the post-war period. Most countries experienced an upturn in fertility from around 1942. In the countries of Western Europe this was generally followed by a slight decline from the late 1940s to the early or mid-1950s, with a further upturn from then until the mid-1960s. In Australia, Canada, New Zealand and the United States fertility rose fairly steadily from the early 1940s. The second major turning point occurred around 1965, when fertility rates began to decline in almost all OECD countries. The main exceptions to the general pattern are: Japan, where fertility has declined almost continuously from the late 1940s, apart from a stabilisation from the early 1960s to the early 1970s; Ireland, where the fertility rate only began to decline in the early 1970s; and Turkey, where fertility has declined only slowly over the post-war period and remains at a relatively high level.

The decline in fertility halted in many countries towards the end of the 1970s, and there were some signs of a reversal of the trend (Chart 2). However, the most recent data indicate a resumption of the decline since the early 1980s in many countries, although in some fertility rates appear to have stabilised at a level slightly above that of the mid-1970s. The long-term decline in fertility since the mid-1960s has led to rates which are very low by historical standards. In most OECD countries the total fertility rates recorded since the mid-1970s are the lowest this century. Fertility is now below the level required for replacement of the population, a total fertility rate of 2.1, in all countries except Ireland and Turkey.

At present, fertility is lowest in a group of European countries, including Austria, Germany, Denmark, Italy, Luxembourg, the Netherlands and Switzerland. The total fertility rate in 1983 was close to 1.5 in most of these countries and was below 1.4 in Denmark and Germany. In most other countries the rate was between 1.6 and 1.8, although in Australia, Greece, Portugal and New Zealand it was above 1.9. Iceland, with a rate of 2.2 in 1983 and Ireland with a rate of 2.7 are well above the OECD norm. In Turkey, where the rate is close to 4.0, fertility is still at a level last experienced by most countries around the turn of the century.

An examination of trends in mortality reveals that the pattern of mortality decline described earlier continued

Table 2. **Life expectancy**

Years

| | At birth | | | | At age 60 | | | |
| | Females | | Males | | Females | | Males | |
	1950	1980	1950	1980	1950	1980	1950	1980
Australia	71.7	78.2	66.5	70.9a	18.5	22.1	15.3	17.2
Austria	67.3	76.1	62.2	69.0	17.6	20.4	15.3	16.4
Belgium	69.0	76.6a	63.8	69.9a	17.8	20.6c	15.6	16.0c
Canada	70.5	79.0	66.3	71.0	18.6	23.0	16.5	18.0
Denmark	71.7	77.4	69.2	71.2	18.0	21.7	17.2	17.0
Finland	68.1	77.6	61.4	69.2	17.0	20.7	14.2	15.6
France	69.7	78.4	63.9	70.2	18.5	22.4	15.4	17.3
Germany	68.3	76.8	64.4	69.7	17.5	20.9	16.3	16.5
Greece	66.6	77.6	63.4	73.1	18.0	21.7	16.2	19.0
Iceland	73.6	80.5	68.7	73.6	20.4	23.5	17.7	19.5
Ireland	67.1	75.0	64.5	69.5	16.1	18.8	15.4	15.5
Italy	67.9	77.7	64.3	71.0	18.5	21.3b	16.9	17.1b
Japan	60.8	79.1	57.5	73.6	16.5	22.3	14.1	18.5
Luxembourg	65.7	75.3	61.7	69.9	16.9	19.8	15.0	15.1
Netherlands	72.8	79.5	70.5	72.5	18.5	22.8	17.8	17.5
New Zealand	71.1	75.6	67.4	69.9	18.4	20.9a	16.0	16.4a
Norway	73.4	79.4	70.0	72.4	19.3	22.5	18.1	17.8
Portugal	61.3	74.2	56.1	67.3	18.1	20.0	15.5	16.0
Spain	64.3	78.0a	59.8	71.8a	17.1	21.3b	14.9	17.6b
Sweden	72.4	79.1	69.9	72.8	18.1	22.3	17.1	17.9
Switzerland	71.3	79.1	66.9	72.3	18.3	22.5	16.1	17.9
United Kingdom	71.3	76.8	66.5	70.7a	18.2	20.8	15.1	16.2
United States	71.2	77.5	65.6	69.5	18.6	22.4b	15.8	17.2b
Average change 1950 - 1980	+ 8.5		+ 5.9		+ 3.5		+ 1.1	

a) 1979; b) 1978; c) 1977.

Sources: OECD, *Living Conditions in OECD Countries*; Paris, 1986, Tables 1.1 and 1.5 and World Health Organisation, *World Health Statistics*, Geneva, various years.

during the post-war period, with the largest decline occurring at younger ages. These trends are reflected in the data on life expectancy shown in Table 2. Between 1950 and 1980, life expectancy at birth increased, on average, by 8.5 years for females and by almost 6 years for males. The increase at age 60 was considerably less, 3.5 years for females and 1.1 years for males. In a number of countries, mortality rates among older males actually rose or remained static in the 1950s and 1960s, but there have been further reductions in most countries since 1970[3]. Since life expectancy of females has risen more rapidly than that of males, the gap between average male and female lifespans has widened over time, although there has been a stabilisation or even a slight narrowing in some countries in recent years. In 1980, average life expectancy at birth was 77.6 years for females and 70.9 years for males, while life expectancy at age 60 was 21.5 years and 17.1 years respectively.

By comparison with fertility and mortality, international migration has been a relatively minor element in overall population change in most OECD countries over the post-war period, although it has had a substantial impact on the labour force in some countries. The high demand for labour in the more advanced OECD economies in the 1950s and 1960s led to inflows of migrants from the less industrialised OECD regions and from developing countries[4]. Countries where migration was relatively important include Australia, Canada, France, Germany, New Zealand and Switzerland, which all registered large inflows in the 1950s and 1960s, and Ireland and Portugal, which experienced substantial outflows. Following the economic downturn from around 1973, international migratory flows were considerably reduced and there was also some reversal of earlier patterns, with a return of migrants from a number of industrialised European countries to some of the less industrialised areas.

This review of past demographic change has shown that the progressive ageing of OECD populations during this century is attributable primarily to declining fertility rates. With the exception of the major upturn from the early 1940s to the mid-1960s and slight fluctuations since the late 1970s, fertility has fallen continuously in most countries since the last quarter of the nineteenth century, thereby transforming the age structure of populations. Mortality and migration have also decreased significantly, but their impact on age distribution has generally been less than that of fertility changes.

The future age distribution of populations will be determined partly by the relative size of existing age cohorts. For example, the large cohorts born during the post-war baby boom represent a sizeable demographic bulge which is gradually working its way through the age structure. Changes in age distribution will also depend on future fluctuations in fertility rates, changes in mortality at different ages, and the level and age structure of international migration. Prospects for the development of these factors are taken up in the next chapter.

Chapter 2

PROJECTED DEMOGRAPHIC TRENDS TO 2050

The OECD Secretariat has recently completed a set of demographic projections for Member countries up to 2050. These projections, which start from 1983, provide an internationally comparable set of calculations of the age and sex structure of populations at five-year intervals. The projections are based partly on assumptions about future fertility rates, mortality rates and international migration provided by national statistical offices, and partly on assumptions devised by the Secretariat. Three principal sets of projections have been made, incorporating varying assumptions about fertility trends, under unchanging assumptions about mortality and migration. These are referred to respectively as the high fertility, medium fertility and low fertility variants. A fourth set of projections, based on a different mortality assumption and using the medium variant fertility assumption, has been made for the seven major OECD countries. This is referred to as the low mortality variant.

The discussion which follows is based mainly on the medium fertility variant, since this is thought to represent the most likely demographic trend in the medium term and to provide a reasonable benchmark assumption for the longer term. The other variants are designed to illustrate the sensitivity of the projections to changes in the underlying assumptions. The variants chosen are by no means exhaustive, the intention being to indicate the effects of a plausible range of deviations from the medium fertility variant rather than to explore the consequences of extreme cases.

Reliability of Demographic Projections

The reliability of projections depends on the accuracy of the assumptions on which they are based and the sensitivity of the projections to variations in the assumptions. The future course of fertility is very uncertain. There have been two major reversals in the trend since the early 1940s and projections of fertility rates have, in the past, proved notoriously unreliable. While the convergence of fertility patterns across OECD countries in the post-war period suggests that some common economic or social factors may be at work, there is considerable controversy over the underlying causes of

fertility behaviour and the likely future trend[5]. If the post-war upturn in fertility rates is regarded as an anomaly in the long-term decline in fertility, then it might be assumed that rates will remain close to their present low levels. But it might also be conjectured that the prospect of shrinking populations would induce a return to replacement-level rates. And if the post-war baby boom were to be regarded as evidence of a long-term cyclical tendency in fertility behaviour, then it might be reasonable to assume that there would eventually be another major upturn in the rates. Because of the uncertainty about future fertility changes, demographic projections generally incorporate several variant fertility assumptions.

Mortality assumptions can be considered more reliable in the short and medium term, because mortality rates have changed gradually in the past and have generally followed a clear downward trend. Given that infant mortality rates and death rates at younger ages are now very low in most OECD countries, the main potential for future change is at the upper end of the age range, with the possibility that further reductions in mortality at older ages will accelerate the ageing of populations. Since it is difficult to predict how rapidly and to what extent life expectancy at older ages may increase in the future, long-term projections of mortality rates may be subject to considerable error.

Future trends in international migration are also uncertain, with past movements providing little guidance. Migratory flows can vary widely over quite short periods of time and future movements are likely to be heavily influenced by policy decisions. However, the uncertainty in this area is much less important than that surrounding fertility projections since migration has been a minor element in population change for most countries in recent decades.

The most reliable population projections relate to people already born because they are unaffected by fertility changes. For example, projections of the working-age population, the 15-64 age group, can be made with reasonable certainty up to the beginning of the next century, since the people who will be in this age group to to 2001 have already been born and mortality rates for the group are low. The main uncertainty with respect to the size of this age group concerns migration rates.

Similarly, the number of people aged 65 and over up to 2050 will be unaffected by fertility rates, although long-term projections of the older age group are sensitive to errors in projected mortality rates. Projections of the numbers of young people are open to error even in the short term, since the size of the younger age groups depends mainly on birth rates.

While absolute numbers of elderly persons can be projected with a reasonable measure of confidence quite far into the future, the proportion of elderly in the total population is much less certain, given that projections of total population size are increasingly determined by fertility rates as the projection period progresses. Similarly, the ratio of elderly to working age people becomes increasingly uncertain after the turn of the century, because birth rates will exert a progressively greater influence on the size of the working age population beyond that point.

Projections of Fertility, Mortality and Migration Rates

At present, most OECD countries project continuing low fertility in the medium term, with either a stabilisation at existing levels or a slight rise. This assumption has been incorporated in the medium fertility variant population projections up to 1995. The majority of countries appear to regard the rate currently prevailing in their country as a minimum level, since only those which still have relatively high fertility (Iceland, Ireland and Turkey) project a further substantial decline.

Beyond 1995 the medium fertility variant assumes a gradual convergence of fertility rates to replacement level, a total fertility rate of 2.1, by 2050. This benchmark assumption reflects a belief that the present low levels of fertility are unlikely to persist over a long period of time and that the average level will eventually settle at the rate required to maintain a constant population. It also reflects a belief that the decline in fertility over the past two decades is closely associated with irreversible social changes, particularly changes in the economic role of women and the increased availability and use of contraceptives, and that fertility is therefore unlikely to return to the high levels experienced in the 1950s and early 1960s.

The high fertility variant assumes that total fertility rates will converge to 2.5 by 2050, implying a return to above replacement-level fertility, although not to such high levels as those experienced during the post-war baby boom. The low fertility variant assumes that fertility rates will converge to 1.4 by 2050, implying that the lowest rate currently prevailing in the OECD area represents a possible point of general convergence and that levels lower than this are unlikely. These high and low variants do not necessarily represent extreme cases since the final values chosen are within the range of recent experience and the rate of convergence to these values is very gradual.

The same mortality assumptions have been used with all three fertility variants. These are referred to as the baseline mortality assumptions. The projections provided by all countries have assumed a flattening out of mortality trends, with three countries – Denmark, Luxembourg and Spain – assuming constant rates. Consequently, projected gains in average life expectancy are quite modest compared with gains over the past decade or so. Life expectancy at birth is, on average, assumed to increase by two years for each sex between 1983 and 2030 and to remain constant for the remainder of the projection period. This contrasts with the average increase of 2.6 years for females and 2.1 years for males experienced in the period from 1970 to 1980. The gap between male and female life expectancy has stabilised or even decreased slightly in over half of the OECD countries since the mid-1970s, although in the remaining cases it has continued to widen. Reflecting this, the mortality assumptions assume a stabilisation or further slight narrowing of the gap in half of the countries over the projection period and a further widening of the gap in the remainder.

As noted earlier, the main uncertainty with respect to future mortality trends concerns changes in life expectancy at older ages. In the past, gains in life expectancy have often been underestimated, and there could be further significant increases in the average life span over the coming decades. As indicated by Table 2, there are substantial differences in average life expectancy in OECD countries at present, suggesting that further gains could be made in a number of cases. It is also possible that advances in medical technology and adoption of healthier lifestyles may lead to further substantial reductions in mortality at older ages. Such a development, in conjunction with persistent low fertility rates, could add discernably to the ageing of populations over the long term. For the purposes of testing the sensitivity of the projections to a more optimistic mortality assumption, a low mortality variant has been projected for the seven major OECD countries. This retains the medium variant fertility rate assumption and the assumptions concerning mortality rates at ages below 60, but it assumes an increase of ten years in life expectancy at age 60 for each sex between 2000 and 2030 and stabilisation thereafter.

The migration assumptions incorporated in the projections generally imply either an approximate continuation of recent relatively low levels of net migration or zero net migration, reflecting the uncertainty surrounding future changes in immigration policy in OECD countries. Such technical assumptions are not in any way intended as statements of future policy directions. Policy with regard to immigration has changed significantly in the past and may change again in the future. For example, population ageing will reduce the size of the working age population in many countries in the decades to come and it is possible that, as in the past, some countries may seek to redress shortfalls in the supply of labour through encouragement of immigration.

Projected Trends in the Growth Rate and Age Structure of Populations

Between 1950 and 1980 the total population of the OECD area increased from 566 million to 780 million, an average annual growth rate of almost 1.1 per cent. As shown in Table 3, the growth rate fell from an annual average of 1.1 per cent in the decade 1950-1960 to 0.8 per cent in the decade 1970-1980, reflecting the general decline in birth rates. By the second half of the 1970s a few countries – Austria, Germany and Switzerland – had begun to experience a decrease in the total population.

As indicated by Table 3, the decline in population growth rates is projected to accentuate in the coming decades, although in most countries population growth is expected to continue up to the end of the century. After that it is projected that an increasing number of countries will experience population decline and that by the end of the projection period only four countries – Australia, Canada, Turkey and the United States – will still have growing populations. The average annual growth rate of OECD populations is projected to decline from 0.5 per cent in the decade 1980-1990 to -0.3 per cent in the decade 2040-2050.

Slowing population growth will be accompanied by significant changes in age structure. The evolving age distributions in the seven major OECD countries are illustrated by Chart 3, while data for all OECD countries are contained in Annex A (Table A.2). The medium fertility variant projections indicate a further marked ageing of populations. Between 1980 and 2040, when the ageing trend is projected to peak, the average proportion aged 65 and over is projected to rise from 12.2 per cent to 21.9 per cent, whereas the average proportion under age 15 is projected to decline from 23.4 per cent in 1980 to 18.3 per cent by 2050, and the average proportion of working age people is projected to decline by about four percentage points.

The above projections are based on the assumption of a return to replacement-level fertility by 2050. The implications of the alternative low and high fertility assumptions for population growth and age structure are summarised in Table 4. The most obvious effect of different fertility paths is on the proportion of young people. Under the low fertility assumption, the proportion of children in the population would be approximately five percentage points lower than under the medium fertility assumption by the end of the projection period, while under the high fertility assumption it

Table 3. **Average annual population growth rates**[a], 1950-2050

Per cent

	1950-1960	1960-1970	1970-1980	1980-1990	1990-2000	2000-2010	2010-2020	2020-2030	2030-2040	2040-2050
Canada	2.7	1.8	1.2	1.0	0.9	0.7	0.6	0.4	0.3	0.3
France	0.9	1.1	0.6	0.4	0.2	0.1	0.0	–0.1	–0.2	–0.3
Germany	0.7	1.3	0.2	–0.1	–0.2	–0.6	–0.7	–0.8	–0.7	–0.8
Italy	0.8	0.6	0.6	0.0	–0.1	–0.2	–0.4	–0.4	–0.5	–0.7
Japan	1.1	1.1	1.1	0.5	0.4	0.1	–0.2	–0.3	–0.2	–0.2
United Kingdom	0.4	0.6	0.1	0.1	0.1	0.1	0.1	0.0	–0.2	–0.2
United States	1.7	1.3	1.1	0.9	0.66	0.5	0.5	0.3	0.2	0.4
Average of above[b]	1.2	1.1	0.7	0.4	0.3	0.1	–0.0	–0.1	–0.2	0.2
Australia	2.3	2.0	1.6	1.3	1.1	0.9	0.7	0.7	0.5	0.5
Austria	0.2	0.5	0.1	0.0	0.1	–0.0	–0.0	–0.2	–0.3	–0.4
Belgium	0.6	0.5	0.2	0.0	–0.1	–0.1	–0.1	–0.2	–0.4	–0.4
Denmark	0.7	0.7	0.4	–0.1	–0.3	–0.4	–0.6	–0.6	–0.6	–0.7
Finland	1.0	0.4	0.4	0.3	0.0	0.0	–0.2	–0.4	–0.5	–0.4
Greece	1.0	0.6	0.9	0.2	0.2	0.2	–0.1	–0.2	–0.3	–0.4
Iceland	2.0	1.5	1.1	1.0	0.6	0.4	0.2	0.2	0.1	–0.2
Ireland	–0.5	0.4	1.4	0.9	0.56	0.4	0.3	0.3	0.2	–0.4
Luxembourg	0.6	0.8	0.7	0.4	0.2	0.0	0.0	–0.1	–0.2	–0.1
Netherlands	1.3	1.3	0.8	0.5	0.3	0.0	–0.2	–0.2	–0.5	–0.5
New Zealand	2.2	1.7	1.1	0.9	0.8	0.5	0.4	0.2	–0.1	–0.2
Norway	1.0	0.8	0.5	0.3	0.2	0.0	0.0	0.0	–0.1	–0.2
Portugal	0.7	–0.1	0.4	0.7	0.3	0.1	–0.1	–0.2	–0.4	–0.5
Spain	0.9	1.1	1.0	0.6	0.3	0.1	0.0	0.0	–0.2	–0.3
Sweden	0.7	0.7	0.3	0.0	–0.04	–0.1	0.0	–0.1	–0.2	–0.2
Switzerland	1.4	1.4	0.2	0.3	0.08	–0.1	–0.3	–0.5	–0.6	–0.6
Turkey	2.9	2.5	2.3	2.7	1.8	1.4	1.1	1.2	0.9	0.4
OECD average[b]	1.1	1.0	0.8	0.5	0.33	0.2	0.1	0.0	–0.2	–0.3

a) 1950-1960 to 1970-1980 actual rates; 1980-1990 to 2040-2050 projected rates.
b) Unweighted average.
Source: Annex A, Table A.1

18

Chart 3

AGE DISTRIBUTION IN THE SEVEN MAJOR OECD COUNTRIES
1950-2050

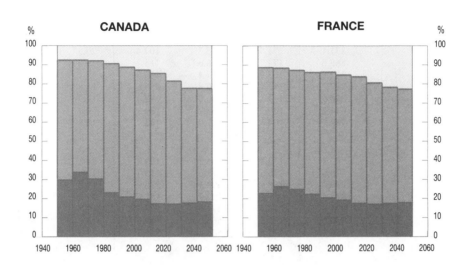

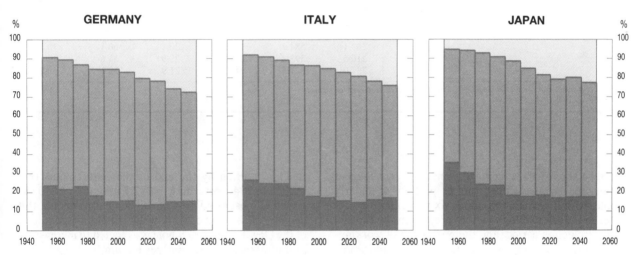

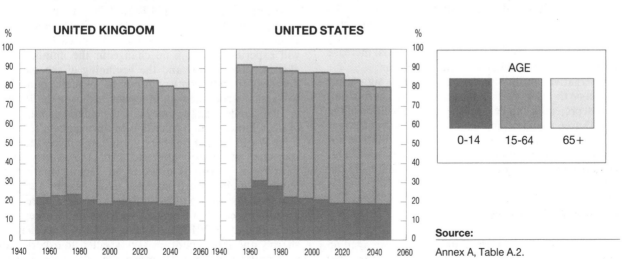

Source:

Annex A, Table A.2.

Table 4. **Variant population projections for the OECD area[a], 1980-2050**

	Total	Number aged			Percentage aged		
		0-14	15-64	65 +	0-14	15-64	65 +
		Millions					
1980	**780.2**	**181.9**	**507.7**	**90.6**	**23.4**	**64.4**	**12.2**
Low fertility							
1990	831.1	173.5	555.3	102.4	20.5	66.6	13.0
2000	869.0	174.7	578.6	115.7	19.3	66.8	13.9
2010	892.3	163.9	597.4	130.9	17.1	67.4	15.4
2020	897.1	152.1	589.4	155.6	15.8	65.9	18.3
2030	878.9	137.5	563.0	178.4	14.9	63.3	21.8
2040	843.2	120.2	533.7	189.3	13.7	62.1	24.2
2050	788.7	104.0	502.0	182.7	12.9	62.2	24.9
Medium fertility							
1990	831.4	173.8	555.3	102.4	20.5	66.6	13.0
2000	870.9	176.6	578.6	115.7	19.5	66.6	13.9
2010	898.0	168.6	598.5	130.9	17.8	66.9	15.3
2020	915.4	167.1	592.7	155.6	17.2	65.0	17.9
2030	925.8	173.4	574.0	178.4	17.7	61.8	20.5
2040	930.0	175.6	565.0	189.3	17.9	60.2	21.9
2050	926.1	175.2	568.2	182.7	18.3	60.6	21.2
High fertility							
1990	831.2	173.6	555.3	102.4	20.5	66.6	13.0
2000	870.9	176.6	578.6	115.7	19.5	66.7	13.9
2010	902.5	173.6	598.0	130.9	18.0	66.7	15.3
2020	933.4	183.6	594.2	155.6	18.5	63.9	17.6
2030	965.7	203.1	584.2	178.4	20.1	60.1	19.8
2040	999.2	216.5	593.4	189.3	20.9	58.6	20.5
2050	1035.5	231.0	621.8	182.7	21.9	59.1	19.0

a) Absolute numbers are totals for the 24 OECD countries; percentages are unweighted averages.
Source: OECD Demographic Data File.

would be about four percentage points higher. Different fertility paths also affect the proportion of elderly people, with a variation of about six percentage points between the low and high variant projections by the end of the projection period, and the proportion of working-age people, with a gap of about three percentage points between the low and high variant projections. The crucial point is that even under the assumption of a return to relatively high fertility rates over the long term, the projections still indicate a substantial increase in the proportion of elderly in the population.

Alternative fertility paths also have a significant impact on the overall size of the population. The medium variant projection implies that the total population of the OECD area would be approximately 19 per cent larger by the end of the projection period than in 1980. The low fertility assumption reduces this growth to one per cent, while the high fertility assumption increases it to 33 per cent.

Trends in the Elderly Population

As shown in Table 4, the numbers of those aged 65 and over are projected to rise from 90.6 million in 1980 to 115.7 million by the end of the century and 189.3 million in 2040, returning to 182.7 million by 2050. The period of most rapid growth will be the second and third decades of the next century when the elderly population of the OECD area as a whole is expected to increase at a rate of about 1.6 per cent per annum.

The more detailed data in Table 5 show that a quarter of the OECD countries, including Austria, Belgium, Denmark, Norway, Sweden and the United Kingdom, will experience very little change in the numbers of elderly between now and the beginning of the second decade of the next century. A number of these countries will actually register a slight reduction during the 1980s or 1990s, reflecting the entry into the elderly population of the relatively small cohorts born during and after the First World War. Elsewhere, quite large increases are projected, particularly after the turn of the century. The most rapid growth is expected in Japan, where the numbers of elderly are projected to increase by 125 per cent in the period up to 2010. Relatively large increases are also expected in Canada, Australia and Turkey. In the period after 2010, the ageing trend will accelerate sharply and most countries are expected to experience substantial increases in the size of the elderly population

Table 5. **Population aged 65 and over**[a], 1950-2050

Millions

	1950	1980	1990	2000	2010	2020	2030	2040	2050
Australia	0.7	1.4	1.9	2.2	2.6	3.4	4.3	4.9	5.0
Austria	0.7	1.2	1.1	1.1	1.3	1.5	1.7	1.7	1.5
Belgium	1.0	1.4	1.4	1.4	1.5	1.7	1.9	2.0	1.8
Canada	1.1	2.3	3.0	3.7	4.5	6.1	7.7	7.9	7.7
Denmark	0.4	0.7	0.8	0.7	0.8	0.9	1.0	1.0	0.9
Finland	0.3	0.6	0.7	0.7	0.8	1.1	1.1	1.0	1.0
France	4.8	7.5	7.7	8.7	9.4	11.2	12.5	12.7	12.2
Germany	4.7	9.6	9.5	10.2	11.5	11.5	12.6	12.5	10.2
Greece	0.5	1.3	1.2	1.5	1.7	1.8	1.9	2.0	2.0
Iceland	0.0	0.0	0.0	0.0	0.0	0.0	0.1	0.1	0.1
Ireland	0.3	0.4	0.4	0.4	0.5	0.5	0.6	0.8	0.8
Italy	3.8	7.7	7.9	8.7	9.6	10.3	11.2	11.7	10.3
Japan	4.4	10.7	14.0	19.4	24.0	26.4	24.4	27.2	26.1
Luxembourg	0.0	0.1	0.1	0.1	0.1	0.1	0.1	0.1	0.1
Netherlands	0.8	1.6	1.9	2.1	2.3	2.8	3.3	3.4	3.0
New Zealand	0.2	0.3	0.4	0.4	0.5	0.6	0.8	0.9	0.9
Norway	0.3	0.6	0.7	0.7	0.7	0.8	0.9	1.0	0.9
Portugal	0.6	1.0	1.2	1.4	1.5	1.6	1.9	2.0	1.9
Spain	2.0	4.1	5.1	5.9	6.5	7.0	8.1	9.2	9.0
Sweden	0.7	1.4	1.5	1.4	1.4	1.7	1.8	1.7	1.6
Switzerland	0.5	0.9	1.0	1.1	1.3	1.6	1.7	1.6	1.4
Turkey	0.7	2.1	2.3	3.5	4.4	6.2	8.8	11.0	13.0
United Kingdom	5.4	8.3	8.5	8.3	8.4	9.5	11.3	11.8	10.6
United States	12.4	25.7	30.4	32.2	35.8	47.4	58.9	61.3	60.7

a)   1950 to 1980 actual numbers; 1990 to 2050 projected numbers.
Source: Annex A, Table A.1.

as the large cohorts born after the Second World War begin to reach age 65.

An examination of the relative weight of the elderly age group within the total population (Table 6) shows that under the medium fertility variant the proportion aged 65 and over is projected to rise fairly slowly in most countries between now and the second decade of the next century, reaching an average of 13.9 per cent in 2000 and 15.3 per cent in 2010. Between 2010 and 2040, however, the proportion is projected to increase rapidly, reaching almost 22 per cent, with a slight decline in many countries thereafter.

Although patterns of population ageing vary quite considerably across countries, it is possible to identify some broad trends. In eight countries, Belgium, Iceland, Ireland, Norway, Sweden, Turkey, the United Kingdom and the United States, the proportion of elderly is projected to increase by less than two percentage points between 1980 and 2010. Indeed the proportion is projected to decline slightly over this period in the United Kingdom, while in many of the other countries mentioned a decline is projected in the 1980s or 1990s. In a second group, including Australia, Austria, Denmark, France, Greece, Italy, the Netherlands, New Zealand and Portugal, an increase of between two and four percentage points is projected between 1980 and 2010. In several of these countries also, the proportion of elderly is projected to decline in the 1980s or 1990s. After 2010 rapid population ageing is projected in both of the above groups of countries. In the remainder, the

onset of rapid ageing is expected much sooner. In Canada, Finland, Germany, Luxembourg and Spain, the proportion of elderly is projected to increase by about five percentage points between 1980 and 2010. In Switzerland an increase of almost seven percentage points is projected and in Japan the projected increase is nine percentage points, representing a doubling of the proportion of elderly. In all countries, further increases are projected between 2010 and 2030 or 2040.

Throughout the OECD area the proportions aged 65 and over in 2040 are projected to be appreciably higher than in the mid-1980s. As at present, the Northern and Western European countries are projected to have the highest proportions of elderly, generally between 23 and 25 per cent of the total population, and exceeding 27 per cent in Germany and 28 per cent in Switzerland. The projected levels for Canada and Japan are over 22 per cent, while for Australia, the United Kingdom, the United States and most of the Southern European countries, it is projected that the elderly will comprise about 20 per cent of the population. Only Turkey, with a projected 10 per cent of the population in the elderly age group, and Ireland with 17 per cent, will still have relatively youthful populations.

The above projections are based on the assumption of relatively modest gains in life expectancy over the coming decades. Table 7 illustrates the impact of the more optimistic low mortality assumption on the projections for the seven major OECD countries. As explained earlier, this variant assumes a gain of ten years in life

Table 6. **Percentage of population aged 65 and over**[a], **1980-2050**

	1980	1990	2000	2010	2020	2030	2040	2050
Canada	9.5	11.4	12.8	14.6	18.6	22.4	22.5	21.3
France	14.0	13.8	15.3	16.3	19.5	21.8	22.7	22.3
Germany	15.5	15.5	17.1	20.4	21.7	25.8	27.6	24.5
Italy	13.5	13.8	15.3	17.3	19.4	21.9	24.2	22.6
Japan	9.1	11.4	15.2	18.6	20.9	20.0	22.7	22.3
United Kingdom	14.9	15.1	14.5	14.6	16.3	19.2	20.4	18.7
United States	11.3	12.2	12.2	12.8	16.2	19.5	19.8	19.3
Average of above countries[b]	12.5	13.3	14.6	16.4	18.9	21.5	22.8	21.6
Australia	9.6	11.1	11.7	12.6	15.4	18.2	19.7	19.4
Austria	15.5	14.6	14.9	17.5	19.4	22.8	23.9	21.7
Belgium	14.4	14.2	14.7	15.9	17.7	20.8	21.9	20.8
Denmark	14.4	15.3	14.9	16.7	20.1	22.6	24.7	23.2
Finland	12.0	13.1	14.4	16.8	21.7	23.8	23.1	22.7
Greece	13.1	12.3	15.0	16.8	17.8	19.5	21.0	21.1
Iceland	9.9	10.3	10.8	11.1	14.3	18.1	20.1	21.1
Ireland	10.7	11.3	11.1	11.1	12.6	14.7	16.9	18.9
Luxembourg	13.5	14.6	16.7	18.1	20.2	22.4	22.0	20.3
Netherlands	11.5	12.7	13.5	15.1	18.9	23.0	24.8	22.6
New Zealand	9.7	10.8	11.1	12.0	15.3	19.4	21.9	21.3
Norway	14.8	16.2	15.2	15.1	18.2	20.7	22.8	21.9
Portugal	10.2	11.8	13.5	14.1	15.6	18.2	20.4	20.6
Spain	10.9	12.7	14.4	15.5	17.0	19.6	22.7	22.9
Sweden	16.3	17.7	16.6	17.5	20.8	21.7	22.5	21.4
Switzerland	13.8	14.8	16.7	20.5	24.4	27.3	28.3	26.3
Turkey	4.7	4.0	5.0	5.5	7.0	8.9	10.2	11.5
OECD average[b]	12.2	13.0	13.9	15.3	17.9	20.5	21.9	21.2

a) 1980 actual proportions; 1990 to 2050 projected proportions.
b) Unweighted average.
Source: Annex A, Table A.2.

Table 7. **Projections of the elderly and very elderly population under variant mortality assumptions**

	Canada	France	Germany	Italy	Japan	United Kingdom	United States
	\multicolumn{7}{c}{% of population aged 65 and over}						
1980	**9.5**	**14.0**	**15.5**	**13.5**	**9.1**	**14.9**	**11.3**
Baseline mortality[a]							
2000	12.8	15.3	17.1	15.3	15.2	14.5	12.1
2020	18.6	19.5	21.7	19.4	20.9	16.3	16.2
2040	22.5	22.7	27.6	24.1	22.7	20.4	19.8
2050	21.3	22.3	24.5	22.6	22.3	18.7	19.3
Low mortality[a]							
2000	12.8	15.3	17.1	15.3	15.2	14.5	12.1
2020	20.0	21.2	23.5	20.7	22.9	18.7	17.2
2040	29.2	29.7	34.1	29.1	29.2	26.4	25.3
2050	33.0	34.0	36.2	31.0	33.1	28.7	29.0
	\multicolumn{7}{c}{% of population aged 80 and over}						
1980	**1.8**	**2.9**	**2.6**	**2.2**	**1.4**	**2.7**	**2.3**
Baseline mortality[a]							
2000	2.8	3.3	3.7	2.7	2.5	3.2	2.9
2020	4.2	5.0	5.4	4.6	4.5	3.3	3.1
2040	7.0	6.9	7.3	5.5	5.6	5.1	5.7
2050	7.2	7.3	8.9	6.4	6.4	5.9	6.0
Low mortality[a]							
2000	2.8	3.3	3.7	2.7	2.5	8.2	2.9
2020	5.5	6.5	6.9	5.8	5.9	4.3	4.0
2040	13.9	14.1	13.9	10.6	11.8	10.3	11.1
2050	19.7	20.0	21.6	15.2	17.0	15.5	16.0

a) "Baseline" and "low" mortality refer to the mortality assumptions described above in the sub-section "Projections of fertility, mortality and migration rates". The medium variant fertility
assumption has been used in all cases.
Source: OECD Demographic Data File.

Table 8. **Trends in the age structure of the elderly population in OECD countries[a], 1980-2050**

	1980	1990	2000	2010	2020	2030	2040	2050
% of population 65 +								
65-69	34.1	32.7	30.8	32.1	31.7	30.8	26.7	26.0
70-79	47.7	45.6	47.5	44.5	46.5	45.6	47.1	43.4
80 and over	18.2	21.7	21.8	23.5	21.9	23.6	26.2	30.7
Millions								
65-69	29.8	33.0	34.4	39.7	47.0	50.7	46.3	43.7
70-79	41.3	44.3	52.7	55.9	67.9	76.9	81.7	71.5
80 and over	15.9	20.9	23.1	28.6	31.8	39.0	47.4	51.6

a) Unweighted average of 21 countries; Finland, Portugal and Turkey excluded; 1980 actual values; 1990 to 2050 projected values.
Source: Annex A, Table A.3.

expectancy at age 60 between 2000 and 2030, implying a major reduction in mortality at older ages. Such a development would lead to a significantly greater increase in the proportion of elderly in the population than that projected on the basis of the more conservative mortality assumptions used in the other variants. By the end of the projection period the percentage aged 65 and over in each country would be between eight and twelve percentage points higher than under the baseline mortality/medium fertility variant.

The general ageing of populations will be accompanied by ageing of the elderly population itself. This trend is summarised in Table 8. In 1980, on average, 34.1 per cent of the elderly in OECD populations were aged between 65 and 69, 47.7 per cent were in the 70-79 age group and 18.2 per cent were aged 80 or over. By 2050 the comparable percentages are projected to be 26.0 percent, 43.4 per cent and 30.7 per cent respectively, indicating an appreciable increase in the proportion of very elderly. Trends in the proportion of very elderly also differ from trends in the elderly population as a whole. Whereas the overall proportion of elderly in the population is not projected to rise very much in many OECD countries before about 2010, the elderly population will itself age markedly well before this. At present the most rapidly growing segment of the elderly population is the group aged 80 and over, whose weight in the population aged 65 and over is projected to increase from an average of 18.2 per cent in 1980 to 21.7 per cent in 1990. Further increases in the proportion of very elderly are expected in the first decade of the next century, followed by a fall between 2010 and 2020, reflecting the movement of large cohorts into the younger segment of the elderly population. But the proportion of very elderly will begin to rise again during the third decade of the next century as these large cohorts grow older. The absolute numbers of very elderly are projected to grow throughout the projection period, increasing by approximately 45 per cent between 1980 and 2000 and more than trebling between 1980 and 2050.

The detailed country data shown in Annex A (Table A.3) indicate that these broad OECD averages mask considerable cross-national variations in the timing of increases in the proportion of very elderly. However, all countries will have to plan for substantial increases in the numbers of very elderly, as well as for fluctuations from decade to decade in the weight of this group in the elderly population.

As may be seen from Table 7, long term projections of the very elderly population are particularly sensitive to assumptions about mortality at older ages. Under the low mortality variant the proportion of persons aged 80 and over in the seven major OECD countries would increase between sixfold and twelvefold between 1980 and 2050. Under the baseline mortality assumptions the projected increases are appreciably lower. Admittedly the assumptions used in the low mortality variant appear highly optimistic in the light of current mortality rates. Nevertheless, the projections serve to underline the fact that rapid progress in reducing mortality at older ages would lead to substantial increases in the numbers and proportions of elderly and very elderly.

The sex composition of the elderly population is of considerable importance for social policy since the needs of men and women in this age group tend to vary significantly. Elderly women figure disproportionately among the more vulnerable elderly groups, with a relatively heavy reliance on basic income support programmes and social services. As a result of their higher life expectancy (Table 2) women outnumber men significantly in the elderly population in OECD countries and

Table 9. **Projected sex composition of population aged 65 and over in OECD countries[a]**

	1980	2000	2030	2040	2050
Number of men per 100 women aged					
65-69	81.9	87.5	89.7	90.7	90.6
70-79	71.2	71.3	76.3	78.2	78.4
80 and over	51.2	47.2	53.0	53.2	53.9

a) Unweighted average of 21 countries; Finland, Portugal and Turkey excluded; 1980 actual ratio; 2000 to 2050 projected ratios.
Source: OECD Demographic Data File.

the sex imbalance increases with age. In 1980 there were, on average, 82 men for every hundred women aged 65-69 and 71 men per hundred women aged 70-79 (Table 9). In the 80-plus age group women outnumbered men by practically two to one. As a result of the assumed stabilisation or slight narrowing of this difference in life expectancy in many countries, the imbalance is, on average, projected to lessen somewhat over time, particularly at the younger end of the elderly age group. Nevertheless, the projections indicate that women will continue to constitute a substantial majority of the elderly and that the sex imbalance within the most elderly age group will remain particularly marked.

Trends in the Working-age Population

Population ageing also has important implications for the size and age structure of the working population. The 1960s and 1970s saw rapid growth in the numbers of working-age people in many OECD countries as the large cohorts born during the period of high fertility from the early 1940s to the mid-1960s reached working age. As shown in Table 10, this growth is already tapering off in many countries, reflecting the decline in fertility from the mid-1960s. By the end of this century, a number of countries, including Austria, Belgium,

Denmark, Germany, Greece, Italy, Japan, Luxembourg and Switzerland, are expected to show a decrease in the absolute number of working-age people. After the turn of the century, the projections indicate that progressively larger numbers of countries will begin to experience shrinkage of the working-age population, particularly during the second and third decades, when the impact of low fertility rates on the numbers of entrants will be compounded by the exit of large cohorts from the working-age group to the elderly age group. By the decade 2020-2030, the numbers of working-age people are projected to be falling in almost all OECD countries, the only exceptions being Australia and Turkey, although, as shown in Table 4, these projections are increasingly sensitive to fertility rate variations as the projection period is extended. After 2030, the rate of decline is projected to decrease, reflecting the impact of the assumed upturn in birth rates towards replacement level. The average proportion of the population in the working-age group is projected to increase from 64.4 per cent in 1980 to 66.6 per cent in 1990 and 69.9 per cent by 2010. After this it is projected to decline, reaching 60.6 per cent by 2050 (Table 4). Again, the exact timing of changes will vary between countries. Details are shown in Annex A (Table A.2).

The average age of the working-age population is projected to rise appreciably over the coming decades as

Table 10. **Growth rate of working-age population**[a], **1950-2050**

	1950-1960	1960-1970	1970-1980	1980-1990	1990-2000	2000-2010	2010-2020	2020-2030	2030-2040	2040-2050
Canada	2.0	2.3	2.1	1.1	0.8	0.7	0.0	−0.3	0.2	0.3
France	0.3	1.1	0.8	0.7	0.2	0.3	−0.4	−0.5	−0.5	−0.3
Germany	0.8	0.7	0.6	0.4	−0.5	−0.7	−0.9	−1.7	−1.1	−0.5
Italy	0.9	0.3	0.6	0.6	−0.2	−0.3	−0.6	−1.0	−1.1	−0.5
Japan	1.9	1.9	0.9	0.9	−0.1	−0.5	−0.4	−0.2	−0.6	−0.2
United Kingdom	0.1	0.3	0.3	0.4	0.0	0.2	−0.1	−0.3	−0.2	−0.1
United States	0.9	1.6	1.7	0.8	0.8	0.7	0.0	−0.2	0.2	0.2
Average of above[b]	1.0	1.2	1.0	0.7	0.1	0.1	−0.4	−0.6	−0.4	−0.1
Australia	1.7	2.2	2.0	1.6	1.1	0.9	0.4	0.3	0.3	0.5
Austria	0.1	−0.3	0.5	0.5	−0.1	−0.1	−0.3	−0.8	−0.5	−0.1
Belgium	0.0	0.3	0.6	0.2	−0.1	0.0	−0.4	−0.8	−0.6	−0.4
Denmark	0.7	0.8	0.4	0.3	−0.1	−0.5	−1.0	−1.2	−1.2	−0.6
Finland	0.9	1.0	0.6	0.3	0.1	−0.2	−1.0	−0.9	−0.5	−0.5
Greece	1.2	0.3	0.9	0.7	−0.1	0.0	−0.1	−0.4	−0.5	−0.4
Iceland	1.2	1.8	1.8	1.4	1.1	0.8	0.0	−0.5	−0.3	−0.3
Ireland	−0.9	0.6	1.4	1.3	1.3	0.8	0.2	−0.1	−0.2	−0.2
Luxembourg	0.2	0.4	1.1	0.4	−0.2	0.1	−0.4	−0.6	−0.2	0.0
Netherlands	0.9	1.6	1.4	0.9	0.1	0.0	−0.6	−1.0	−0.8	0.0
New Zealand	1.6	1.9	1.7	1.5	0.9	0.6	0.1	−0.4	−0.4	−0.2
Norway	0.5	0.7	0.6	0.6	0.4	0.2	−0.4	−0.5	−0.49	−0.10
Portugal	0.6	−0.2	0.6	1.2	0.2	0.2	−0.1	−0.6	−0.68	−0.47
Spain	0.7	0.8	1.1	1.0	0.4	0.4	−0.1	−0.6	−0.76	−0.35
Sweden	0.6	0.7	0.1	0.2	0.1	−0.2	−0.4	−0.4	−0.41	−0.10
Switzerland	1.2	1.3	0.5	0.6	−0.2	−0.4	−0.8	−1.0	−0.82	−0.45
Turkey	2.4	2.3	2.7	3.4	2.2	2.0	1.3	0.7	0.71	0.75
OECD average[b]	0.8	1.0	1.0	0.9	0.3	0.2	−0.3	−0.5	−0.43	−0.17

a) Average annual compound growth rates; 1950-1960 to 1970-1980 actual rates; 1980-1990 to 2040-2050 projected rates.
b) Unweighted average.
Source: Annex A, Table A.1.

Table 11.   **Projected trends in age structure of the working-age population in OECD countries**[a]

	1980	1990	2000	2010	2020	2030	2040	2050
% of population 15-64 aged:								
15-19	13.3	11.1	9.9	9.7	9.0	9.2	10.0	10.0
20-24	12.5	12.0	9.8	9.6	9.4	9.2	9.8	10.1
25-44	42.2	44.8	44.8	40.7	39.3	40.1	39.4	39.5
45-54	17.4	17.2	20.1	21.5	21.6	20.1	21.2	20.0
55-64	14.6	14.9	15.6	18.4	20.7	21.4	19.7	20.3

a)   Unweighted average of 24 OECD countries; 1980 actual values; 1990 to 2050 projected values.
Source: OECD Demographic Data File.

a result of decreases in the proportion of entry level workers. This trend is summarised in Table 11, which shows that the average proportion of younger working-age people (15-24) is projected to decline from 26 per cent in 1980 to 20 per cent in 2000 and 18 per cent by 2030, rising again to 20 per cent in 2050. The proportion in the middle age groups (25-44) is expected to rise from 42 per cent in 1980 to 45 per cent in 2000 and to decline quite sharply, to 39 per cent, by 2040; the proportion aged 45-64 is projected to increase appreciably, from 32 per cent in 1980 to 36 per cent in 2000 and 41 per cent in 2030, falling back to 40 per cent in 2050. In each of the seven major OECD countries it is projected that more than one in five of the working-age population will be aged 55 or over by 2020, and Germany and Japan are expected to have already reached this situation by the turn of the century.

Trends in the Young Population

The proportion of young people in the population is projected to fall quite sharply up to about 1990 (Table 12). Thereafter, the projected decline is more gradual as the assumed movement of fertility towards replacement level begins to affect birth rates. By the

Table 12.   **Percentage of population aged 0-14**[a]

	1980	1990	2000	2010	2020	2030	2040	2050
Canada	23.0	20.8	19.5	17.2	17.0	17.5	18.1	19.0
France	22.3	20.4	19.2	17.4	17.0	17.4	17.9	18.2
Germany	18.2	15.1	15.5	13.2	13.4	14.9	15.2	16.7
Italy	22.0	17.8	17.1	15.4	14.6	16.0	17.0	17.7
Japan	23.5	18.3	17.5	18.3	16.8	17.3	17.4	17.3
United Kingdom	21.1	19.1	20.5	19.9	19.9	19.0	17.9	18.8
United States	22.5	21.8	21.1	19.3	19.2	18.9	18.9	19.2
Average of above[b]	21.8	19.0	18.6	17.3	16.9	17.3	17.5	18.1
Australia	25.3	22.2	21.5	19.9	19.2	19.1	19.0	19.2
Austria	20.5	18.1	18.8	17.0	16.8	17.2	17.3	18.2
Belgium	20.0	18.8	18.3	16.6	16.3	16.8	17.3	18.1
Denmark	20.9	16.8	15.8	14.7	14.0	15.5	16.6	17.6
Finland	20.3	19.2	17.5	15.8	15.7	16.4	17.2	17.9
Greece	22.8	20.3	18.9	18.0	17.3	17.2	17.2	17.4
Iceland	27.5	25.1	21.7	18.8	17.7	18.4	19.0	18.9
Ireland	30.5	27.5	23.2	21.1	20.1	20.4	20.7	19.7
Luxembourg	18.8	17.5	17.7	16.1	16.6	17.2	17.5	18.6
Netherlands	22.3	18.1	18.2	16.4	15.8	16.3	16.3	17.2
New Zealand	27.0	22.3	21.2	19.4	18.0	17.5	17.1	17.5
Norway	22.2	18.7	18.5	17.3	16.6	17.2	17.5	18.0
Portugal	26.8	22.4	21.4	19.7	18.3	18.2	18.0	17.7
Spain	25.9	21.7	19.8	16.8	15.9	17.2	18.0	18.0
Sweden	19.6	17.2	17.4	16.9	16.3	17.0	17.4	18.0
Switzerland	19.7	16.7	16.4	14.8	14.5	14.9	15.1	16.2
Turkey	39.1	35.8	32.1	27.4	25.1	26.3	26.0	22.6
OECD average[b]	23.4	20.5	19.5	17.8	17.2	17.7	17.9	18.3

a)   1980 actual value; 1990-2050 projected values.
b)   Unweighted average.
Source: Annex A, Table A.2.

second decade of the next century the proportion of young people is projected to stabilise or begin rising slightly again in most countries. As may be seen from Annex A (Table A.1), the actual number of young people is projected to continue rising in all of the non-European OECD countries except Japan throughout the period up to 2050. In most European countries the trend in the absolute size of the young population follows the trend in its relative size.

Notwithstanding the similarity of trends across Member countries, there is quite a large range of variation in the proportion of the population in the young age group. Generally speaking, the Northern and Western European countries, where fertility rates have in many cases now reached very low levels, have the smallest proportions of young people, ranging from 18 per cent in Germany to 22 per cent in France, Italy, the Netherlands and Norway. In Canada, Japan, Greece and the United States the young comprise about 23 per cent of the population, while in the remaining Southern European countries, and in Australia and New Zealand, they comprise between 26 per cent and 27 per cent. Iceland with 27.5 per cent of the population in the 0-14 age group, Ireland with 30.5 per cent, and

Turkey with 39 per cent have very large young populations by OECD standards. Similar cross-national variations are evident in the projected proportions of young people in 2050, with the range going from 16.2 per cent in Switzerland to 22.6 per cent in Turkey.

NOTES AND REFERENCES

1. See, for instance, Laslett, Peter, "Societal Development and Aging" in Robert H. Binstock and Ethel Shanas (eds.), *Handbook of Aging and the Social Sciences* (second edition), New York, Van Nostrand Reinhold Company, 1985, pp. 199-230.

2. See Ermisch, John F., *The Political Economy of Demographic Change*, London, Heinemann, 1983, Table 1.5.

3. OECD, *Living Conditions in OECD Countries*, Paris, 1986, Table 1.5.

4. See OECD, *Demographic Trends 1950-1990*, Paris, 1979.

5. See Easterlin, R.A., *Birth and Fortune, the Impact of Numbers on Personal Welfare*, London, Grant McIntyre, 1980 and Ermisch, *op.cit.*

SUMMARY OF PART I

Current population projections indicate that all OECD countries will have to plan for growth in the numbers of elderly and very elderly persons, as well as for marked increases in the weight of the elderly in the total population over the next half century. The ageing of populations also implies a decline in the relative weight of the young and working-age populations and, in many cases, shrinkage in the absolute size of these groups as well as in the size of the total population. The ageing trend is further reflected in projected changes in the age structure of the working-age population, with an appreciable increase projected in the proportion of older workers.

These demographic developments are determined by past and projected changes in fertility, mortality and international migration rates. In view of what has been said about the difficulty of predicting future fertility trends, the elements of the projections which are heavily dependent on fertility assumptions must be considered very tentative. However, in some important respects projected shifts in the age structure are a result of changes in demographic variables which have already taken place. Thus, it is not until after the end of the century that future fertility trends will begin to affect the absolute size of the working age population and different fertility paths will have no impact on the size of the elderly population. Fertility developments will exert a progressively greater influence on the overall age structure of the population as the projection period

progresses, the birth rate being inversely related to the weight of the elderly within the total population. However, even in the event of an upturn in fertility rates towards replacement level or higher in the second and third decades of the next century, the passage into old age of the large number of people born between the early 1940s and mid-1960s will lead to an appreciable ageing of populations. With mortality rates at younger ages now very low in most OECD countries, the main potential for further reductions is at older ages. A reduction in mortality among the elderly would of course increase their proportion in the population.

Changes in the age structure of populations have important implications for the demand for social transfers and services, for the capacity of society to finance social programmes, for the distribution of resources among different age groups in the population, and for labour supply and labour force structure. Increases in the absolute numbers of elderly and changes in their distribution by age and sex also have important social policy implications, affecting the demand for income support, for a range of social services and for employment. Moreover, there is a high rate of turnover in the elderly population, and the changing characteristics and needs of successive cohorts of elderly persons may have a significant impact on social policy requirements in the future. These social and labour market issues are taken up in subsequent chapters.

Part II

THE IMPLICATIONS OF AGEING POPULATIONS FOR SOCIAL EXPENDITURE

INTRODUCTION

Age is one of the principal factors determining the nature and extent of an individual's social needs. The very young require physical care and protection. Educational requirements and the duration of schooling are measured largely in terms of the student's age. Age is a major determinant of retirement decisions and the consequent requirement for income support, and with increasing age the demand for health care and personal support services rises steeply. Employees at the beginning and end of their working life are more susceptible to unemployment than those in mid-career, and many other risks, such as invalidity, are also correlated with age. Earning potential and the capacity to support oneself and contribute to the support of others is also related to age.

Social needs are met in a variety of ways, through public programmes, voluntary community services, family networks, private sector initiatives and the individual's own resources. The mix of services varies from country to country, but in all OECD countries public sector provision has assumed a major role. Consequently, changes in the age structure of populations have important implications for the demand for various types of public social programmes.

The ageing of populations is likely to increase the demand for pensions, for health care and for other social services catering to the needs of the elderly, while demographic pressure on education systems and other services utilised mainly by the young may decrease. Changes in the absolute and relative size of the working age population are a major determinant of the size of the labour force, which in turn will affect the capacity to finance social programmes.

The key social policy concern arising out of current demographic trends is whether the ageing of populations is likely to lead to a major increase in the cost of public social programmes and whether society, and in particular the working population, will be able or willing to bear the additional financing burden. Chapter 3 takes up the issue at a purely demographic level, examining projected trends in the numbers of young and elderly compared to trends in the numbers of working-age people. This approach, which defines people as dependants or workers on the basis of age alone, provides an initial indication of the magnitude and timing of changes in the dependency burden due to shifts in the age structure of populations.

However, the impact of demographic change on social dependency burdens is not simply a function of the relative size of different age groups. The level of public social expenditure on individuals of different ages is also of crucial importance in determining the evolution of costs. Thus, Part II is essentially devoted to establishing the pattern of social expenditure across the various age groups, to assessing on this basis the likely impact of population ageing on the level and structure of social expenditure in selected OECD countries up to the year 2040, and to examining the consequences for the evolution of the financing burden.

It must be emphasized that the results presented in this part are projections and not predictions of the impact of demographic change on future expenditure trends and dependency burdens. The analysis is based on the population projections set out in Part I and is, therefore, subject to the same uncertainty about future demographic changes. Moreover, since the primary concern here is the impact of population ageing, a range of other factors which will influence the growth of social expenditure have been either set aside or included only for the purpose of illustrating alternative scenarios. Thus, no attempt is made to predict how demands or policies may change in the future, although such changes are likely to have an important influence on expenditure trends. Nor is any attempt made to predict how the economic climate may change in the coming decades. Projections of the financing burden are based purely on projected changes in the working age population, although the sensitivity of the projections to variations in the demographic and social policy assumptions is illustrated.

A note of caution must also be entered concerning the cross-national comparability of the projections. The basic social expenditure data for the analysis are taken from a series compiled by the OECD, which are reasonably consistent across countries. However, neither tax expenditures nor private sector social expenditure are included in the calculations. Since the importance of both varies considerably from country to country, this affects the ratio of public social expenditure to GDP, the distribution of public expenditure across the different age groups and the projected growth in expenditure due to population ageing. In countries where tax expenditures constitute an important form of social expenditure, the projections will only partially reflect the implications of a changing age structure for public social outlays. And where the private sector plays a large role in the provision of social services, the projections will understate the impact of demographic change on the total dependency burden. Finally, estimates of the pattern of social expenditure across different age groups are based partly on national sources and partly on calculations by the OECD Secretariat, and are not fully consistent across countries. For all of these reasons caution must be exercised in comparing expenditures across countries. The primary objective of the analysis is to project expenditure trends over time within countries.

Chapter 3

TRENDS IN DEMOGRAPHIC DEPENDENCY RATIOS

In OECD countries the major proportion of social expenditure flows to the young and the elderly, while outlays on those in the working-age groups are much lighter. But it is principally the working-age groups, or more accurately the employed population, which provide the resources to finance social programmes through social security contributions and taxes. Since social programmes are, therefore, important instruments of redistribution between age groups, projected trends in the ratio of working age persons to young and elderly persons in a population provide a convenient first order indication of the impact of population change on the social support burden. This ratio is known as the dependency ratio. For the purpose of calculating dependency ratios, it has been assumed that all those in the 15 to 64 age group are economically active and contributing to the support of the dependent segments of the population, and that all those under age 15 and over age 64 are dependent for support on transfers of resources from the working population.

Dependency ratios calculated in this way do not, of course, represent the actual support burden at any given point in time since they ignore age- and sex-specific variations in labour force participation rates and unemployment rates. And since participation rates and unemployment rates vary between countries, these

Table 13. **Total dependency ratios in OECD countries, 1980-2050**[a]

	1980	1990	2000	2010	2020	2030	2040	2050	% Change	
									1980-2040	2010-2040
Canada	48.1	47.4	47.9	46.6	55.3	66.5	68.4	67.7	42	47
France	56.8	51.8	52.6	50.8	57.3	64.4	68.3	68.2	20	34
Germany	50.8	44.0	48.3	50.5	54.3	68.7	74.8	69.9	47	48
Italy	54.9	46.1	47.9	48.6	51.5	61.1	69.9	67.6	27	44
Japan	48.4	42.2	48.6	58.6	60.6	59.5	66.8	65.7	38	14
United Kingdom	56.2	51.9	53.8	52.7	56.7	61.9	62.1	60.2	10	18
United States	51.1	51.6	49.8	47.2	54.6	62.4	63.1	62.5	23	34
Average of the above	52.3	47.9	49.9	50.7	55.8	63.5	67.6	66.0	29	34
Australia	53.5	49.9	49.5	48.2	52.9	59.5	63.0	63.0	18	31
Austria	56.2	48.5	50.9	52.5	56.7	66.6	70.2	66.5	25	34
Belgium	52.4	49.2	49.3	48.0	51.6	60.2	64.4	63.7	23	34
Denmark	54.5	47.3	44.3	45.7	51.8	61.5	70.3	68.9	29	54
Finland	47.7	47.8	46.8	48.4	59.9	67.1	67.7	68.5	42	40
Greece	56.1	48.3	51.3	53.3	54.1	58.0	61.9	62.6	10	16
Iceland	59.8	54.8	48.2	42.9	46.9	57.5	64.3	66.7	7	50
Ireland	70.0	63.5	52.4	47.3	48.5	54.1	60.2	63.2	−14	27
Luxembourg	47.8	47.3	52.6	52.0	58.1	65.6	65.3	63.4	37	26
Netherlands	51.1	44.5	46.3	46.1	53.1	64.8	69.6	66.2	36	51
New Zealand	58.0	49.4	47.6	45.7	50.0	58.4	63.8	63.4	10	40
Norway	58.5	53.6	50.7	47.9	53.3	61.0	67.4	66.4	15	41
Portugal	58.6	52.1	53.7	51.1	51.4	57.3	62.3	62.0	6	22
Spain	58.1	52.5	51.9	47.8	49.0	58.4	68.4	69.0	18	43
Sweden	56.0	53.7	51.5	52.5	59.0	63.2	66.4	65.0	19	26
Switzerland	50.5	46.1	49.6	54.6	63.6	73.1	76.5	73.7	52	40
Turkey	78.1	65.9	59.1	49.0	47.3	54.3	56.7	51.9	−27	16
OECD average	55.6	50.4	50.2	49.5	54.1	61.9	66.3	65.7	19	35

a) [Population (0-14) + (65+)/population 15-64] × 100; 1980 actual ratios; 1990 to 2050 projected ratios.
Source: Annex A, Table A.1.

dependency ratios are not suited to making cross-national comparisons of dependency burdens at a given point in time. The utility of demographic dependency ratios lies in the fact that they allow the impact of demographic change on the dependency burden over time to be isolated from other, non-demographic, factors such as variations in labour force participation rates, unemployment rates and levels of social benefits.

The total dependency ratio measures the number of elderly (65+) and young (0-14) persons relative to the number of working-age persons (15-64). Separate youth and aged dependency ratios can also be calculated. Projections to 2050 of total dependency ratios in OECD countries, based on the medium fertility variant projections set out in Part I, are shown in Table 13. On average, the total dependency ratio is projected to increase by 19 per cent between 1980 and 2040, when it generally peaks. A more substantial rise, 29 per cent, is projected for the seven major OECD countries. There is considerable variation between countries, with the ratio projected to decline in Ireland and Turkey, to increase by 10 per cent or less in Greece, Iceland, New Zealand, Portugal and the United Kingdom, and to increase by over 30 per cent in Canada, Finland, Germany, Japan, Luxembourg, the Netherlands and Switzerland. This longer-term trend masks the fact that the ratio has been falling in almost all OECD countries since the 1970s, a trend which is expected to continue in the medium term and which reflects the impact of declining numbers of child dependants and the relatively small size of the cohorts now approaching and entering old age. Only in six countries – Austria, Germany, Greece, Japan, Luxembourg and Switzerland – is the ratio expected to rise substantially again before 2010.

After 2010, however, a substantial rise in the ratio is projected for virtually all countries as the proportion of elderly in the population increases. The exceptions to this pattern are Turkey, where the ratio is projected to continue falling until after 2020, and Greece, Ireland, Portugal and Spain, where it is not projected to rise significantly until after 2020. The projected increases in Japan and the United Kingdom in the period 2010-2040 are also relatively small. Particularly large increases are projected in Canada, Denmark, Finland, Germany, Iceland, Italy, the Netherlands, New Zealand, Norway, Spain and Switzerland, where the dependency burden is expected to rise by 40 per cent or more between 2010 and 2040.

Chart 4 illustrates the sensitivity of projections of the total dependency ratio to variations in fertility assumptions. Within the range of fertility assumptions used in the Secretariat's projections, the average dependency ratio across the seven major OECD countries in 2050 varies by about 14 per cent, from 61.6 dependants per 100 working-age persons under the low fertility variant to 70.1 under the high fertility variant. Under all three fertility assumptions the dependency ratio is projected to rise quite sharply after 2010.

Trends in the total dependency ratio mask an impor-

Chart 4

PROJECTED TOTAL DEPENDENCY RATIO UNDER ALTERNATIVE FERTILITY ASSUMPTIONS

(Average for the seven major OECD countries)

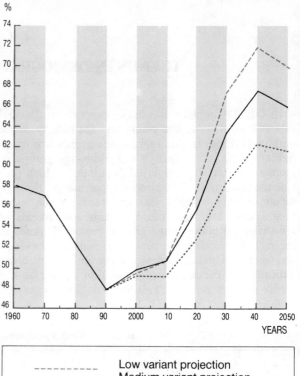

----------	Low variant projection
——————	Medium variant projection
··················	High variant projection

Source:

OECD Demographic Data File.

tant divergence in the youth and aged dependency ratios. As a consequence of population ageing, the elderly will comprise an increasing proportion of the dependent population in the coming decades, while the proportion of young dependants is expected to decline. In 1980, an average 35 per cent of those in the dependent age groups in OECD countries were elderly persons; by 2050, the average proportion of elderly dependants is projected to have risen to 54 per cent. This shift in the age composition of the dependent population is clearly reflected in the contrasting trends in the youth and aged dependency ratios in the seven major countries shown in Chart 5. Under the medium fertility assumption the youth dependency ratio declines quite sharply up to

Chart 5

PROJECTED YOUTH AND AGED DEPENDENCY RATIOS
UNDER ALTERNATIVE FERTILITY ASSUMPTIONS

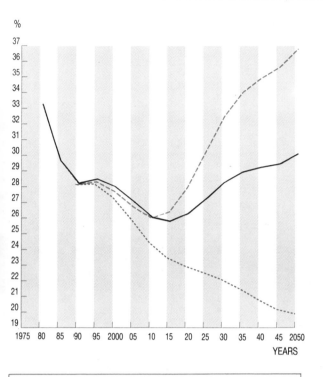

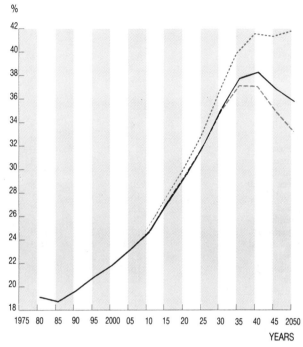

	Youth dependency ratio Average for seven major countries
....	Low variant projection
————	Medium variant projection
– – – –	High variant projection

	Aged dependency ratio Average for seven major countries
....	Low variant projection
————	Medium variant projection
– – – –	High variant projection

Source:

OECD Demographic Data File.

1990, falls more gradually after that, and begins to rise again in the second decade of the next century, reflecting the assumption of a gradual return to replacement level fertility. A similar pattern is projected for the OECD area as a whole, with the average ratio projected to decline from 37 young dependants per 100 working age persons in 1980 to 26 per 100 in 2020, increasing to 30 per 100 in 2050. By contrast, the average aged dependency ratio in the seven major countries is projected to increase from 17 per 100 in 1980 to 32 per 100 in 2040. Over the OECD area as a whole the average aged dependency ratio is projected to increase from 19 per 100 in 1980 to 37 per 100 in 2040.

Many countries will experience only a slight increase in the aged dependency ratio in the period up to 2010,

and in a third of the countries the ratio will fall before the end of this century (Table 14). Exceptions to this pattern are Japan and Switzerland, where the aged dependency ratio is projected to increase rapidly between now and 2010. Quite large increases are also expected in Canada, Finland, Germany, Greece, Italy, Luxembourg, the Netherlands and Spain. After 2010, all countries will experience rising aged dependency ratios as the large cohorts born after the Second World War begin to enter old age, and in the majority the increase will be relatively large. On average, the number of elderly dependants will increase sharply in the first half of the twenty-first century; measured as the ratio of elderly dependants per working-age person, it is projected to increase by 63 per cent between 2010 and

Table 14. **Aged dependency ratios in OECD countries, 1980-2050**[a]

	1980	1990	2000	2010	2020	2030	2040	2050	% Change	
									1980-2040	2010-2040
Canada	14.1	16.8	19.0	21.4	28.9	37.3	37.8	35.8	168	77
France	21.9	20.9	23.3	24.5	30.6	35.8	38.2	37.6	74	56
Germany	23.4	22.3	25.4	30.6	33.5	43.6	48.2	41.6	106	58
Italy	20.8	20.1	22.6	25.7	29.3	35.3	41.0	37.9	97	60
Japan	13.5	16.2	22.6	29.5	33.6	31.9	37.8	37.0	180	28
United Kingdom	23.2	23.0	22.3	22.3	25.5	31.1	33.1	30.0	43	48
United States	17.1	18.5	18.2	18.8	25.0	31.7	32.3	31.4	89	72
Average of the above	19.1	19.7	21.9	24.7	29.5	35.2	38.3	35.9	108	57
Australia	14.8	16.6	17.5	18.7	23.6	29.0	32.1	31.7	117	72
Austria	24.2	21.7	22.6	26.6	30.4	38.0	40.8	36.2	69	53
Belgium	21.9	21.1	22.0	23.5	26.9	33.3	36.0	34.0	64	53
Denmark	22.3	22.6	21.5	24.3	30.5	36.4	42.1	39.1	89	73
Finland	17.7	19.4	21.2	24.9	34.8	39.8	38.8	38.2	119	56
Greece	20.5	18.2	22.6	25.7	27.4	30.8	34.0	34.2	66	32
Iceland	15.8	16.0	16.1	16.1	20.9	28.5	33.2	35.2	110	106
Ireland	18.2	18.5	16.9	16.3	18.7	22.7	27.1	30.8	49	66
Luxembourg	20.0	21.6	25.5	27.5	31.9	37.1	36.4	33.2	82	32
Netherlands	17.4	18.4	19.7	22.1	28.9	37.8	42.0	37.6	141	90
New Zealand	15.4	16.2	16.3	17.5	23.0	30.7	35.8	34.8	132	105
Norway	23.4	24.9	22.8	22.4	27.9	33.4	38.2	36.4	63	71
Portugal	16.1	17.9	20.8	21.4	23.7	28.7	33.1	33.4	106	55
Spain	17.2	19.4	21.8	23.0	25.3	31.1	38.2	38.6	122	66
Sweden	25.4	27.3	25.1	26.6	33.1	35.4	37.4	35.3	47	41
Switzerland	20.8	21.6	25.0	31.7	39.9	47.2	49.9	45.6	140	57
Turkey	8.5	6.6	8.0	8.2	10.3	13.8	15.9	17.5	87	94
OECD average	18.9	19.4	20.8	22.9	27.6	33.3	36.6	35.1	98	63

a) [Population 65+/population 15-64] × 100; 1980 actual ratios; 1990 to 2050 projected ratios.
Source: Annex A, Table A.1.

2040, declining slightly thereafter. The highest projected aged dependency ratios are in Germany and Switzerland, with 48 and 50 elderly persons respectively per 100 working-age persons in 2040. As at present, the projected ratio in Turkey is far below the OECD average.

Chart 5 demonstrates that within the range of fertility assumptions considered in the Secretariat's projections, alternative fertility paths would have only a slight effect on the development of the aged dependency ratio. Under all three fertility assumptions the ratio increases rapidly between 2010 and 2035. Under the low fertility assumption the ratio then remains more or less constant during the remainder of the projection period, whereas under the other assumptions the ratio declines.

Projections of the youth dependency ratio are very sensitive to variations in the fertility assumptions, although the differences do not become large until well into the next century due to the very gradual approach to the assumed final fertility values. By the end of the projection period the low fertility assumption produces an average ratio of about 20 per 100 in the seven major countries, whereas the high fertility assumption produces a ratio of almost 37 per 100.

Two important points emerge from the foregoing examination of projected dependency ratios. Firstly, although projected reductions in the youth dependency ratios will substantially offset increasing aged dependency ratios, this will not be sufficient to prevent a rise in the total dependency ratio in most countries, particularly between 2010 and 2040. Thus, the ageing of populations implies a quite significant increase in the demographic dependency burden in the majority of cases. The second point concerns the impact on the overall cost of public social programmes of changes in the age structure of the dependent population. Since an increasing proportion of dependants will be elderly persons, the relative levels of social expenditure on the young and the elderly become a matter of crucial importance for the projection of financing burdens. If social expenditures per capita for the young and the elderly are approximately equal, then trends in the total dependency ratio can be taken as a reasonably good guide to changes in the burden on the active population. If, on the other hand, outlays for the young and the elderly are not approximately equal, then it is necessary to take account of the divergent trends in the youth and aged dependency ratios. Of course, considerable shifts in the composition of expenditures can be expected independently of whether the total grows more or less rapidly.

Chapter 4

POPULATION AGEING AND SOCIAL EXPENDITURE

The Distribution of Social Expenditure by Age Groups

Cross-sectional analysis of social expenditure data indicates that public social expenditures display a marked concentration by age group. For example, expenditure on pensions is concentrated on the older age groups, while expenditure on family benefits is concentrated on the young. Expenditure on education is also concentrated on the younger age groups, while expenditure relating to employment and unemployment is concentrated on the active age groups, particularly at the younger and older ends of the working age population. Health care expenditure is less closely linked to age but is relatively high for the elderly, the very young and for women of child-bearing age.

Available data show that, on average, public expenditure on health care is considerably higher for older persons than for the remainder of the population. The estimates shown in Table 15 for twelve OECD countries indicate that per capita public spending on health care for those aged 65 and over is, on average, 4.3 times that

for persons aged under 65. Expenditure on the very elderly is higher still, with per capita outlays for those aged 75 and over exceeding outlays on those under age 65 by an average of 5.9. There is considerable variation in expenditure patterns across countries, with the expenditure ratio for the over-65s ranging from 7.4 in the United States, to 2.2 in Italy, and the ratio for the over-75s ranging from 9.2 in Sweden to 2.8 in France. Care must be exercised in using such data to draw international comparisons. While differences between countries are partially due to variations in the utilisation and delivery of care, the data also reflect differences in the public-private health care mix. For example, the very high ratio shown for the United States is explained by the fact that public health care programmes in that country are primarily directed towards the elderly, with the remainder of the population relying heavily on private provisions. When total (public and private) expenditure is taken into account, the distribution in the United States is less heavily skewed towards the elderly. Finally, the estimates are drawn from a variety of survey and administrative data sources and may not be fully consistent across countries.

When all of the main social programmes are taken into account, it becomes clear that total per capita social outlays on the elderly substantially exceed those on the young. The example shown in Table 16, relating to Australia, shows that at the beginning of the 1980s, total per capita social outlays for those aged 65 and over were 2.7 times higher than per capita outlays on those under age 16. Data relating to the Netherlands, shown in Table 17, reveal a similar pattern, with per capita outlays on the 65 and over age group exceeding spending on those under age 20 by a ratio of 2.7. In both countries, per capita outlays on the very elderly exceed those on the young by an even greater ratio. In Australia, expenditure on those aged 75 and over was 3.4 times greater than that on children under age 16; in the Netherlands, expenditure on those aged 80 and over exceeded that on the under-20s by a factor of almost 4.

Estimates for an additional ten countries, shown in Table 18, indicate a pattern of expenditure very similar to that shown for Australia and the Netherlands. In 1980, per capita outlays on those aged 65 and over

Table 15. **Ratio of per capita public health expenditure on elderly to non-elderly in selected OECD countries**

	Year	Expenditure ratio	
		Persons aged 65+/ Persons aged 0-64	Persons aged 75+/ Persons aged 0-64
Australia	1980/81	4.9	8.0
Canada	1974	4.5	6.7
Denmark	1983	4.1	4.8
France	1980/81	2.4	2.8
Germany	1975	2.6	3.1
Ireland	1979	4.5	6.0
Italy	1983	2.2	–
Japan	1980	4.8	5.3
Netherlands	1981	4.5	6.2
Sweden	1983	5.5	9.2
England	1979/80	4.3	6.6
United States	1978	7.4	–
Average		4.3	5.9a

a) Average of 10 countries.
Source: See Annex B.

Table 16. **Per capita social expenditure by age group: Australia, 1980-81**

Dollars

	0-15	16-24	25-59	60-64	65-69	70-74	75 +
Social security							
Cash transfers	321	340	343	1 569	2 431	2 933	3 136
Welfare services	58	42	10	56	113	143	211
Health	173	229	330	690	866	996	2 262
Education	1 086	825	125	28	32	–	–
Employment	3	80	7	3	–	–	
Total*a*	1 641	1 516	814	2 346	3 442	4 072	5 609

a) Discrepancies between totals and sums of per capita outlays are due to rounding.
Source: Social Welfare Policy Secretariat, *The Impact of Population Changes on Social Expenditure: Projections from 1980-81 to 2021*, Canberra, 1984.

Table 17. **Per capita social expenditure by age group: Netherlands, 1981**

Guilders

	0 - 19	20 - 44	45 - 64	65 - 79	80 +
Social security	1 700	2 190	5 910	12 020	13 350
Education	3 930	560	–	–	–
Health care	790	640	1 060	2 710	7 020
Social services	110	50	130	930	5 010
Total	6 530	3 440	7 100	15 660	25 380

Source: Social and Cultural Planning Office, *Collectieve uitgaven en demografische ontwikkeling, 1970 - 2030*, Rijswijk, 1984.

Table 18. **Per capita social expenditure by age group in selected OECD countries in 1980**

In units of national currency

	0 - 14	15 - 64	65 +	65 + / 0 - 14
Belgium	117 453	74 503	242 017	2.1
Canada	2 462	1 772	6 535	2.7
Denmark	20 589	14 483	42 259	2.1
France	15 529	7 975	40 902	2.6
Germany	5 823	3 464	18 409	3.2
Italy	1 027 334	1 127 477	3 900 727	3.8
Japan	435 874	191 868	1 022 829	2.3
Sweden	20 860	8 974	48 871	2.3
United Kingdom	918	490	1 956	2.1
United States	1 874	1 254	7 135	3.8
Average				2.7

Source: See Annex B.

exceeded outlays on those under age 15 by a ratio of between 2.1 (Belgium, Denmark and the United Kingdom) and 3.8 (Italy and the United States). On average, outlays on the elderly exceeded those on the young by a ratio of 2.7.

While there is evidently considerable variation across countries with respect to age-related expenditure patterns, it is clear that in none of the twelve countries

examined could a one-for-one cost offset be expected between young and elderly dependants. Since per capita expenditures on the elderly substantially exceed those on the young, projected increases in the proportion of elderly and very elderly dependants are likely to lead to an appreciably greater increase in the social dependency burden than that implied by a simple head count of the total number in the dependent age groups.

Methodology for Projecting the Impact of Demographic Factors on Social Expenditure

In view of the variations in social expenditures across age groups, a more accurate representation of the implications of demographic change for social dependency burdens can be achieved by combining information on present per capita social outlays for the different age groups with projections of the size of these age groups. As emphasized earlier, expenditure projections obtained by this method reflect only demographic effects and are in no sense intended as forecasts. In order to isolate the demographic factor, the other influences on social expenditure growth have been set aside. Thus, it is assumed that the average real benefit per capita for those in a given age group remains constant.

By combining data on per capita outlays for different age groups within the various social programmes with population projections, it is possible to show how changes in age structure would alter the size of individual programmes, the distribution of expenditure across the different programmes and age groups, and the level of total social expenditure. The population projections used are those based on the medium fertility variant as set out in Chapter 2. The analysis covers five major social programmes: education, health care, pensions (old age, survivors and permanent sickness), unemployment compensation and family benefits. Housing expenditures have not been included due to lack of information on the age distribution of expenditures and problems of cross-national comparability of expenditure data. A range of income maintenance programmes have been excluded from the analysis for most countries, also due to lack of data on the age distribution of expenditures. The most important of such programmes are temporary sickness and welfare services[1]. Tax expenditures are also excluded, the analysis being confined to direct expenditures. Overall, the programmes included in the analysis represented, on average, 90 per cent of total direct social outlays (excluding housing) in 1980 in the countries analysed.

Twelve countries are included in the analysis. Detailed studies of the age distribution of social expenditure published by the Australian and Dutch authorities have been used as a basis for the analysis for these two countries. For the other ten countries (Belgium, Canada, Denmark, France, Germany, Italy, Japan, Sweden, the United Kingdom and the United States) estimates of the age distribution within the relevant programmes have been made partly on the basis of data supplied by national authorities and partly on the basis of data files maintained by the OECD Secretariat. Details of the data sources and of the calculations of age-expenditure coefficients are provided in Annex B.

The years for which age-specific expenditure data are available vary from country to country, although in all cases efforts have been made to obtain data for 1980 or the nearest year. In order to achieve consistency in the base year for the expenditure projections, the age-expenditure coefficients obtained for the twelve countries have in all cases been applied to expenditure data relating to 1980 for the relevant programmes. Expenditure totals for the relevant programmes have been taken from the OECD Secretariat's social expenditure files, thus ensuring consistency of the data across countries.

Projected Trends in Social Expenditure

The impact of projected changes in the size and age structure of populations on the growth of real social expenditure up to 2040 is shown in Table 19. On the assumption that real per capita benefits for the various age groups remain constant at 1980 levels, the cumulative expenditure growth implied by demographic changes varies widely across the twelve countries examined, ranging from a 107 per cent increase in Australia to a 12 per cent decrease in Denmark. Apart from Australia, countries where a large increase is projected include Canada (87 per cent), Japan (40 per cent) and the United States (65 per cent). Expenditure is projected to decline by 3 per cent in Germany, to remain virtually stable in Belgium and to increase by 10 per cent or less in Italy, Sweden and the United Kingdom. Chart 6 illustrates the projected changes averaged across the twelve countries.

Variations in the projected growth rates of social expenditure are related to differences in total population trends and in the rate of growth of the elderly population. As may be seen from Table 19, countries with the highest projected rates of expenditure growth are also those where both the total population and the elderly population are expanding rapidly. This is the case in Australia, Canada and the United States. The relatively high expenditure growth projected for Japan is attributable almost exclusively to population ageing, as very little change is projected in the total population. In the European countries the projected increases in the elderly population are smaller and are offset by shrinkage or very low growth of the total population.

Changes in the age structure of populations are clearly reflected in the divergent trends projected for expenditures on the different social programmes. Increases in the size of the elderly population imply rapid growth of pension expenditures. In all of the countries examined, the projected growth of outlays on pension programmes substantially exceeds the projected growth rate of total social expenditure, with differences between countries mirroring variations in the growth of the elderly population. Thus, the projected increase in outlays is most marked in the non-European countries. Among the European countries the largest increases are in France and the Netherlands. Expenditure on health care programmes is also projected to increase quite rapidly in the non-European countries, with more modest increases in European countries. While health

Chart 6

PROJECTED CHANGE IN SOCIAL EXPENDITURES DUE TO DEMOGRAPHIC FACTORS 1980-2040

Average of twelve OECD countries[1]

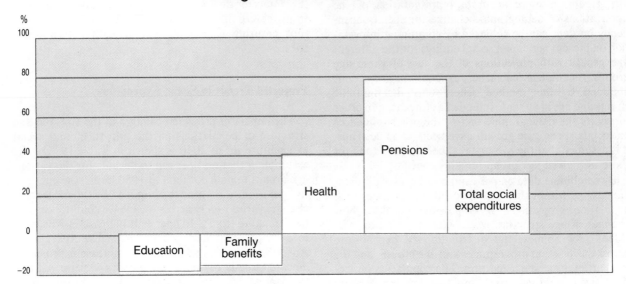

Note:

1. Australia, Belgium, Canada, Denmark, France, Germany, Italy, Japan, Netherlands, Sweden, United Kingdom, United States.

Source:

OECD, Social Data Bank.

Table 19.   **Growth of public social expenditure implied by projected demographic change**[a], **1980-2040**

(1980 = 100)

	Education	Family benefits	Health	Pensions	Total social expenditure[b]	Total population	Population 65+
Australia	128	126	240	288	207	168	346
Belgium	71	74	99	134	102	92	139
Canada	103	110	218	304	187	146	345
Denmark	58	61	95	124	88	77	131
France	80	83	119	172	128	104	170
Germany	53	60	90	126	97	74	131
Italy	62	64	108	134	107	85	152
Japan	79	77	146	229	140	102	255
Netherlands	70	69	137	160	121	98	210
Sweden	83	84	117	123	109	95	126
United Kingdom	85	86	121	130	110	103	141
United States	102	114	178	215	165	136	238

a)   Cumulative growth rates assuming constant real per capita expenditure by age within each programme.
b)   Including education, health, pensions, family benefits, unemployment compensation and, in the case of Australia and the Netherlands, other cash benefits and welfare services.
Sources: Annex A, Table A.1; Annex B, Table B.1.

Table 20. **Shifts in the distribution of social expenditure by major programme and age group implied by projected demographic change[a]**

| | Programmes (%) | | | | | | Age groups (%) | | | | | |
| | Education | | Health | | Pensions | | 0 - 14 | | 15 - 64 | | 65+ | |
	1980	2040	1980	2040	1980	2040	1980	2040	1980	2040	1980	2040
Australia	31	19	25	29	29	40	27	16	45	35	28	49
Belgium	26	18	16	16	40	52	22	17	46	38	32	45
Canada	32	18	29	33	24	38	24	15	50	35	26	50
Denmark	29	19	21	23	30	42	22	15	47	38	31	47
France	21	13	22	21	42	56	24	16	36	31	40	53
Germany	20	11	25	23	47	61	17	10	37	28	46	62
Italy	23	13	24	24	47	59	15	9	50	41	35	50
Japan	31	17	29	30	28	46	32	17	39	31	29	52
Netherlands	23	13	20	23	34	46	22	13	51	38	27	49
Sweden	23	18	31	33	39	44	23	18	32	26	45	56
United Kingdom	28	22	26	29	34	40	24	19	40	33	36	48
United States	32	20	22	24	40	52	21	14	40	30	39	56
Average	27	17	24	26	36	48	23	15	43	34	35	51

a) Assuming constant real per capita expenditure by age within each programme.
Source: Annex B, Table B.2.

care expenditures on the elderly are projected to rise substantially in all twelve countries, the increases are in many cases offset by a projected reduction in expenditures on shrinking young populations. This is most evident in Belgium, Denmark and Germany, where demographic trends imply a reduction in total public health care outlays. With the exception of Australia, Canada and the United States, the young population is projected to shrink in all of the countries analysed. This implies a decrease in demographic pressure on education programmes, with an appreciable reduction projected in the European countries and in Japan. A similar decrease is implied with respect to family benefits. Outlays for education are projected to remain virtually constant in Canada and the United States and to increase by 28 per cent in Australia. Outlays on family benefits are projected to show a modest increase in all three countries.

Table 20 summarises the shifts in the distribution of social expenditure by major programme and age group which are implied by population ageing. On average, the share of expenditure directed to education is projected to decline by almost 40 per cent, from 27 per cent to 17 per cent of the social budget, with particularly large decreases implied in Canada, Germany, Italy, Japan and the Netherlands. Conversely, the share of pension expenditure is projected to rise by a third, on average, with an increase of 64 per cent projected in Japan and an increase of 58 per cent in Canada. The share of health care outlays is projected to rise slightly, on average, going from 24 per cent to 26 per cent of total social expenditure. These projected changes in programme shares imply marked shifts in the flows of social expenditure to the different age groups. The average proportion of social outlays going to the young is projected to fall by over a third on average. Expenditure

on the working-age population is also projected to decline, whereas expenditure on the elderly is projected to rise, on average, by 46 per cent.

The timing of expenditure changes due to demographic factors varies significantly between programmes. Chart 7 shows that in the European countries and Japan, where education expenditure is projected to decline markedly over the period 1980-2040, the major part of this decline occurs in the 1980s and 1990s, with the rate of decline levelling off after the turn of the century. Indeed expenditure is projected to rise slightly again in the early part of the next century in Japan and the United Kingdom. These trends are, of course, a reflection of the effect of the assumed upturn in fertility rates which is incorporated in the population projections. Education expenditure is projected to increase gradually throughout the projection period in Australia, whereas in Canada and the United States a slight decline is projected in the 1980s, with a slight increase again in the first decade of the next century.

In most cases, demographic pressures on pension expenditures are not projected to begin increasing until sometime during the first decade of the next century. Exceptions to this pattern are Germany, where expenditures are projected to start rising in the 1990s, Japan, where a very sharp increase is projected between now and 2010 with a decrease in the growth rate thereafter, and the Netherlands, where the rate of increase is relatively constant throughout the projection period. Expenditure on health care is projected to grow more steadily over the period as a whole, although in a number of countries the rate of growth accelerates after the turn of the century and in many cases it declines towards the end of the projection period.

The analysis so far indicates that the projected shifts in demand for the various social programmes due to

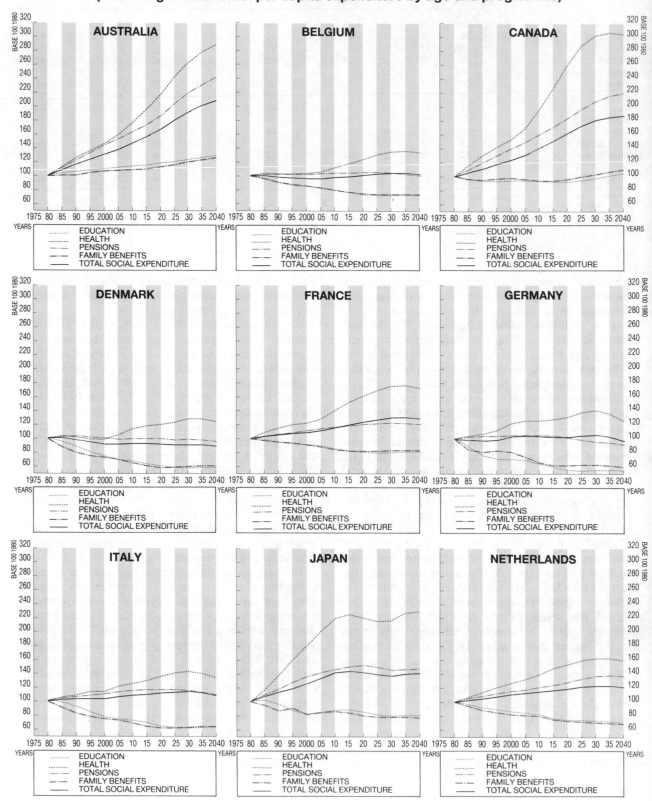

Chart 7

**GROWTH OF SOCIAL EXPENDITURE BY MAJOR PROGRAMME
IMPLIED BY PROJECTED DEMOGRAPHIC CHANGE
1980-2040**
(Assuming constant real per capita expenditure by age and programme)

38

Chart 7 (Cont'd)

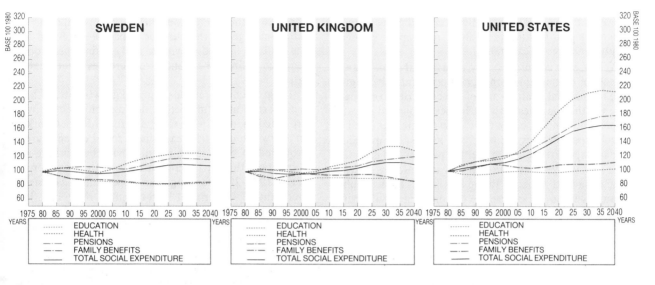

Source:

Annex B, Table B.1.

demographic change are in many cases more significant than the implied increase in aggregate social expenditure. On the basis of current age-specific expenditure patterns, population ageing implies a significant reallocation of resources from programmes serving the young to programmes serving the elderly. To the extent that such a reallocation occurs, the projected increase in total social expenditure is very modest in most European countries, with a decrease in expenditure projected in two cases. The projected increases are more significant in France and the Netherlands and are quite substantial in Australia, Canada, Japan and the United States. All of the countries examined here are likely to face substantial increases in the cost of pension programmes as the numbers of elderly grow. In some countries quite large increases in health care expenditure are implied by changing age structures and in all twelve countries the structure of demand for health care provision will change as a result of increases in the elderly population and decreases in the young. Most countries will also be faced with the problem of adjusting education systems and family benefit programmes to shrinkage in the young population.

The Capacity to Finance Social Expenditure Increases

The rates of growth in GDP necessary to finance the growth in public social expenditure implied by demographic factors are shown in Table 21. If it is assumed that the policy intention is to hold the ratio of social expenditure to GDP at 1980 levels, then the economic growth rates necessary to absorb the effect of demographic change are the same as the implied growth in total social expenditure. In the two countries with the highest projected expenditure growth, Australia and Canada, the necessary GDP growth rates over the period 1980-2040 average out at 1.2 per cent and 1.05 per cent per annum respectively. In the remaining countries the required economic growth rates are under one per cent per annum, with the United States near the

Table 21. **Rate of GDP growth necessary to finance increases in social expenditure due to demographic factors**

	Projected increase in social expenditure 1980-2040 (1980 = 100)	Share of social expenditure in GDP in 1980 (%)	Average annual GDP growth required to maintain social expenditure share constant[a]
Australia	207	18.6	1.22
Belgium	102	38.2	0.03
Canada	187	21.0	1.05
Denmark	88	34.9	−0.22
France	128	28.3	0.41
Germany	97	30.8	−0.05
Italy	107	26.9	0.11
Japan	140	16.9	0.56
Netherlands	121	35.5	0.32
Sweden	109	32.5	0.14
United Kingdom	110	22.0	0.16
United States	165	20.7	0.84

a) Average annual compound growth rates.
Source: Table 19; OECD, *Social Expenditure 1960-1990*, Paris, 1985.

top of the range, Japan and France near the middle and the remaining countries near the bottom. The necessary growth rate is almost zero in Belgium and is negative in Denmark and Germany, where demographic changes imply a decline in expenditure.

When viewed in this way, the social expenditure effects of demographic change appear unlikely to give rise to financial strain in any of the countries examined. Even in the countries with the highest projected rates of expenditure increase, the GDP growth rates required to absorb the increases are relatively modest compared to the average rates achieved over the past several decades. The scenario presented in Table 21 is, however, unrealistic in several respects. In the first place, demographic change will not, of course, be the only factor affecting social expenditure, as has been assumed here. Real social benefit levels have risen substantially in the past and can, for a variety of reasons which will be discussed later, be expected to continue rising in the future. There may also be potential for expansion of the coverage of social programmes, although this factor is unlikely to be as important a source of expenditure growth in the future as it has been in the past. In countries where demographic change pre-empts a significant share of the resources available for social expenditure over the coming decades, the capacity to cope with other sources of expenditure growth will inevitably be limited and programmes are likely to come under financial strain.

Prospects for the various countries must also be viewed in the context of existing levels of social expenditure. Where expenditure shares are already high, as is the case in many European countries, there may be pressure to reduce expenditure, leaving less latitude for coping with demographic change. Conversely, where the expenditure share is relatively low, as in Japan, it may be possible to respond at least partially to demographic pressures by allocating a larger proportion of national resources to social programmes.

A further element which must be taken into account concerns the impact of demographic change on the capacity to finance social expenditure. Since social programmes are financed largely on the basis of taxes and social security contributions paid by the working population, the number of people employed and trends in their real earnings will be key elements in coping with expenditure increases. As shown in Part I, the labour force is affected by demographic change via trends in the size and age structure of the working-age population. Such changes may also have repercussions on the growth of productivity. Thus, leaving aside non-demographic sources of social expenditure growth, a more accurate assessment of the capacity to cope with the pure demographic effect on expenditure requires that prospective trends in the size and productivity of the labour force be taken into account.

As in the case of the expenditure projections presented earlier, some simplifying assumptions will be adopted in order to isolate the effect of demographic change on financing capacity. If it is assumed that aggregate labour force participation rates and unemployment rates remain constant at 1980 levels, then changes in the size of the working age population will reflect changes in the number of people employed and the increase in productivity or real earnings per worker required to finance expenditure increases can be calculated.

Table 22 compares the projected growth rates of total social expenditure implied by demographic factors with projected changes in the expenditure burden per worker. In all twelve countries examined, social expenditure is projected to grow more rapidly than the working-age population, the gap in cumulative growth rates over the period 1980-2040 ranging from 54 per cent in Japan and Germany to 11 per cent in the United Kingdom. This implies that average real earnings per worker would have to increase by a similar amount in order to finance the additional expenditure without recourse to increased tax or social security contribution rates. The required annual average growth in real earnings ranges from 0.72 per cent in Japan and Germany to 0.17 per cent in the United Kingdom.

Prospects for the various countries thus appear in quite a different light when trends in the working age population are taken into account. In the countries where projected growth rates of social expenditure are highest – Australia, Canada and the United States – the working-age population is also projected to grow over the projection period as a whole. This significantly moderates the earnings growth required to finance the additional expenditure. On the other hand, in many of the countries where projected growth rates of expenditure are relatively low, a decline is projected in the working-age population, with the result that real earnings per worker would have to rise more rapidly to keep pace with expenditure. This is the case, for instance, in Denmark and Germany where projected declines in the working-age population are greater than projected declines in social expenditure.

The growth rates in real earnings required to absorb the effects of demographic change represent significant cumulative increases for some countries, although in the case of Belgium, Denmark, Sweden, and the United Kingdom, the required increase is quite low. In all cases the increase would appear to be quite manageable if spread evenly over the sixty year projection period since nowhere does the required average annual growth in earnings exceed 0.7 per cent. Unfortunately, however, the impact of demographic change will not be spread evenly over a long period, but will instead be concentrated over a shorter timespan.

Table 22 shows that in most of the countries examined, expenditure and financing capacity will remain in balance until after the turn of the century. Indeed, in a number of countries projected growth rates of expenditure are below those of the working-age population between now and the early part of the next century, implying some easing of the financing burden. After 2010, however, social expenditure is projected to

Table 22.   **Impact of demographic change on social expenditure and financing burdens – 1980-2040**[a]

	1990	2000	2010	2020	2030	2040
Australia						
Social expenditure	116	130	146	166	190	207
Financing burden per head of 15-64 age group	99	100	103	112	124	130
Belgium						
Social expenditure	98	96	98	101	104	102
Financing burden per head of 15-64 age group	96	95	97	103	116	120
Canada						
Social expenditure	111	124	141	162	181	187
Financing burden per head of 15-64 age group	100	103	109	125	143	145
Denmark						
Social expenditure	97	91	92	91	90	88
Financing burden per head of 15-64 age group	94	88	95	103	115	126
France						
Social expenditure	106	109	116	124	130	128
Financing burden per head of 15-64 age group	99	100	104	116	128	132
Germany						
Social expenditure	98	104	104	103	106	97
Financing burden per head of 15-64 age group	95	106	113	124	149	154
Italy						
Social expenditure	103	103	108	111	113	107
Financing burden per head of 15-64 age group	97	99	106	116	131	139
Japan						
Social expenditure	113	125	141	141	136	140
Financing burden per head of 15-64 age group	103	115	137	142	140	154
Netherlands						
Social expenditure	105	111	115	119	123	121
Financing burden per head of 15-64 age group	96	100	104	114	131	139
Sweden						
Social expenditure	101	98	101	107	111	109
Financing burden per head of 15-64 age group	99	95	100	110	119	122
United Kingdom						
Social expenditure	98	97	101	105	113	110
Financing burden per head of 15-64 age group	95	93	96	101	112	111
United States						
Social expenditure	107	112	125	147	162	165
Financing burden per head of 15-64 age group	99	96	99	117	132	131

a)   Projections.
   Financing burdens are calculated by comparing projected changes in total social expenditure with projected changes in the number of people aged 15-64.
Source: OECD Social Data Bank.

grow more rapidly than the working-age population in Australia, France, Sweden and the United States. A similar situation arises in Canada, Italy, and the Netherlands from around 2005, from the mid-1990s in Germany and from about 1990 in Japan. In Belgium, Denmark and the United Kingdom the projected growth rates of expenditure remain below those of the working-age population until 2015 or 2020.

These data reveal that the ageing of populations creates the potential for considerable pressure with respect to the financing of social programmes during certain parts of the projection period. While expenditure is rising due to the ageing of populations, the number of working age people will be growing only slowly or declining. This is highlighted by Table 23, which compares projected growth rates of social expenditure and

Table 23.   **Implications of projected demographic change for social expenditure financing burden during selected sub-periods**

	Period	Projected compound growth (base year = 100)		Growth in real earnings per worker required to cope with pure demographic effect	
		Social expenditure	Population aged 15-64	Compound growth (base year = 100)	Average annual compound growth %
Australia	2010-2040	142	111	128	0.8
Belgium	2015-2040	103	85	121	0.8
Canada	2005-2040	143	102	140	1.0
Denmark	2015-2040	96	75	128	1.0
France	2010-2040	111	87	128	0.8
Germany	1995-2040	98	63	156	1.0
Italy	2005-2040	101	76	133	0.8
Japan	1990-2040	124	83	149	0.8
Netherlands	2005-2040	108	78	138	0.9
Sweden	2010-2040	108	88	123	0.7
United Kingdom	2020-2040	105	96	109	0.4
United States	2010-2040	133	100	133	1.0

Sources: Annex A, Table A.1; Annex B, Table B.1; OECD Secretariat estimates.

the working-age population during the sub-period when the former overtakes the latter. In all countries except the United Kingdom, projected expenditure growth outstrips growth of the working-age population by at least 20 per cent over the relevant sub-period, with an average gap of 32 per cent across the twelve countries. During these periods the financing of the additional social outlays implied by population ageing will require, on average, an increase of over 0.8 per cent per annum in average real earnings. The highest projected increases, one per cent per annum, are in Canada, Denmark, Germany and the United States. The lowest increases are in the United Kingdom and Sweden, with 0.4 per cent and 0.7 per cent respectively.

To summarise, the analysis so far suggests that even if social expenditures on the young decrease to the full extent implied by demographic change, population ageing will still add significantly to the burden of financing social expenditure from the early part of the next century in most countries examined here. The financing burden is projected to increase much sooner in Germany and Japan. Even where the growth rates of social expenditure implied by demographic factors are quite low, the coincidence of static or declining working-age populations leads to an increase in the burden per worker. Thus, during the periods identified in Table 23, demographic change will require significant additional resources to be directed towards social programmes.

The additional resources required to absorb the effects of demographic change must come from increased productivity per worker, from higher rates of taxes and social security contributions, from a reduction in the scale of coverage and benefits offered by public social programmes, or from some combination of the three. For the purposes of the scenario outlined above, it has been assumed that the additional resources are provided by increases in productivity, with real per capita benefit levels being held constant. Under such an assumption, the growth in real earnings required to cope with the effects of population ageing, although quite substantial, appears manageable in view of growth rates achieved in the past. However, the implication of this assumption is that in order to deal with the financing burden implied by demographic change, a substantial gap would be allowed to open up between the living standards of the working population and the levels of benefits provided in social programmes. Clearly, it is unrealistic to assume that benefit levels can be held constant in real terms over a long period of time. In the past, average benefits have generally risen as fast as or faster than productivity[2]. To the extent that this were to happen in the future, the additional resources required to cope with demographic effects would have to be provided by raising tax and contribution rates, implying a sharp increase in tax burdens during the sub-periods identified earlier. Individual countries will have to choose how to deal with demographic pressures, but whatever the rate of productivity growth, all will be faced with a trade-off between increasing real benefit levels and raising taxes and social security contributions.

Chapter 5

SENSITIVITY OF EXPENDITURE PROJECTIONS TO UNDERLYING ASSUMPTIONS

The above discussion has attempted to isolate the effects of demographic change on public social expenditure and financing burdens on the basis of a number of fairly simplistic assumptions. The chief of these were:

a) that birth and death rates move according to the medium fertility variant projections as shown in Chapter 2;

b) that real per capita social benefits by age within each programme remain fixed at their 1980 levels;

c) that labour force participation rates and unemployment rates remain at their 1980 levels.

Under these conditions it was concluded that:

a) the ageing of populations implies a substantial reallocation of expenditures from social programmes serving the young to those serving the elderly;

b) even in the event that the maximum reallocation implied by demographic change is achieved, social expenditure will still grow significantly in some countries over the next sixty years, although in most European countries the projected increase is very modest.

c) because the working-age population is projected to shrink or to grow only slowly over most of this period, the financing burden per working-age person increases significantly in most countries;

d) this increase in the financing burden will in most cases be concentrated in the period from first decade of the next century up to 2040;

e) the resources required to cope with the effects of demographic change must be obtained from productivity increases, higher rates of taxes and social security contributions, a reduction in the benefits offered by public social programmes (below what might otherwise be possible) or a combination of the three.

The question arises as to the extent to which these conclusions are sensitive to changes in the underlying assumptions and the extent to which the assumptions themselves are likely to be modified by ongoing commitments embodied in social programmes, by changes in social demands, by the growth of the economy, by changes in labour force participation rates, or by explicit or implicit changes in policy. Clearly, any non-demographic influences which lead to an increase in the *scale* of social programmes (relative to, say, GDP) will also increase the importance of demographic change: the two effects are multiplicative rather than additive. On the other hand, scope to deal with demographic problems may be found via a contraction in programme benefits and coverage relative to the growth of productivity or earnings. It should also be noted that any problems encountered in making the appropriate switch in social expenditure from programmes catering for the young to those catering for the elderly will add to the overall pressure on resources. This chapter explores the sensitivity of the projections to changes in the key assumptions with a view to identifying the main policy issues which are likely to arise in the context of coping with demographic change.

Demographic Assumptions

The foregoing analysis was based on the medium fertility variant population projections, assuming a gradual upturn in fertility towards replacement level and an extrapolation of recent mortality trends, with some flattening off of gains in life expectancy towards the end of the projection period. The demographic pressure on social programmes would be altered in two ways should these assumptions prove inaccurate. First, different fertility and mortality trends would change the proportions of young and elderly people in the population. This would affect the relative demands for programmes targeting the two groups, with repercussions on the size and composition of the total social budget. Second, the size of the working-age population would, after a time lag of fifteen years, be progressively affected by different fertility trends, with repercussions on the capacity to finance social programmes.

Table 24 illustrates the effect on the expenditure projections of adopting the low fertility and low mortality assumptions, both of which would lead to greater ageing of populations. Japan and the United Kingdom have been chosen since the first appears to be facing a relatively serious ageing problem while in the second the

Table 24. **Sensitivity of expenditure projections to demographic assumptions**[a]

Demographic assumption	Projected growth 1980-2040 (1980 = 100)[b]					
	Education expenditure	Health expenditure	Pension expenditure	Total social expenditure	Population 15-64	Growth in average real earnings necessary to cope with demographic change
Japan						
Medium fertility/baseline mortality	79	146	229	140	91	154
Low fertility/baseline mortality	56	139	229	128	80	160
Low mortality/medium fertility	79	180	296	169	91	186
United Kingdom						
Medium fertility/baseline mortality	85	121	130	110	99	111
Low fertility/baseline mortality	54	109	130	95	83	114
Low mortality/medium fertility	85	153	168	131	99	132

a) Details of the demographic assumptions are provided in Chapter 2.
b) Assuming constant real per capita expenditure by age within each programme.
Sources: Table 19, Table 22 and OECD Secretariat estimates.

projected demographic pressure is relatively light. The assumptions concerning the economic and social policy parameters are as before. In both cases, the low fertility scenario implies an appreciable additional saving on education expenditure. Additional savings on family benefits, not shown separately here, are also implied. The projected growth rate of health care outlays is also reduced as a result of the lower fertility assumptions. Pension expenditures are not affected. The net impact on the projected growth rate of total social expenditure is quite sizeable. In the case of the United Kingdom, the low fertility assumption implies a reduction of 5 per cent in social expenditure over the projection period as a whole, as compared with the increase of 10 per cent projected under the medium fertility assumption. In the case of Japan, the lower fertility assumption implies a reduction of over 10 per cent in expenditure compared to expenditure under the medium fertility assumption. The crucial point to note, however, is that since the lower fertility assumption also produces a sizeable reduction in the working-age population, the increase in the financing burden is actually higher under this scenario.

Under the low mortality scenario the projected increases in health and pension expenditures are significantly higher than under the baseline mortality assumption, while outlays on education and other programmes serving the young are unaffected. The net result is that in Japan the projected increase in total social expenditure over the period 1980-2040 is 69 per cent and in the United Kingdom 31 per cent, as compared with the increases of 40 per cent and 10 per cent respectively projected under the baseline mortality assumption. The financing burden increases more under this scenario than under the other demographic scenarios shown here. In Japan real earnings per worker would have to grow by 86 per cent over the projection period in order to provide the additional resources necessary to cope with demographic change, while in the

United Kingdom the required increase in earnings is 32 per cent. These increases are appreciably higher than those projected under the baseline mortality assumption.

The above examples demonstrate that the expenditure projections are quite sensitive to variations in the mortality assumptions and a major reduction in mortality rates at older ages would add significantly to demographic pressures on social programmes. The more intensive population ageing implied by a further reduction in fertility rates would also add to the demographic pressure, although the impact is less severe than that of the low mortality scenario.

Economic Assumptions

It is clearly easier for governments to cope with demands for additional social expenditure in the context of a growing economy. In the context of the present study the issue which arises in relation to productivity growth is whether this is itself likely to be affected by the ageing of populations. The impact of projected ageing and shrinkage of the labour force on labour productivity and the rate of technological innovation is uncertain. Nor is it clear how changes in age structure may affect rates of saving and investment. These issues are taken up in Part III.

With respect to the sensitivity of the expenditure projections to the growth rate of productivity, the crucial factor is whether or not real per capita social benefits increase in line with the real earnings of the working population. If real benefit levels change at the same rate as real earnings, then the assumed rate of productivity growth has no effect on the development of the financing burden. The burden per worker will simply be a function of changes in the size of the working population relative to changes in expenditure caused by demographic factors. And under such a scenario any increase in the financing burden would, in terms of existing financing arrangements, have to be met by raising taxation and social security contribution rates.

Table 25 illustrates how variations in the assumed relationship between average real earnings and per capita real benefits affect the development of the financing burden over the period 1980-2040. The projections for Canada and Germany are used as examples and the demographic assumptions are the same as those used throughout this chapter. Four different assumptions are used concerning the relationship between benefits and earnings. In each case, real benefits per capita are assumed to increase at an annual average rate of 3.0 per cent. Real earnings per worker are assumed to increase *i)* at the same annual rate as per capita benefits, *ii)* 0.5 percentage points faster than benefits, *iii)* 1.0 percentage point faster than benefits, *iv)* 1.5 percentage points faster than benefits, yielding increases of 3.0 per cent, 3.5 per cent, 4.0 per cent and 4.5 per cent respectively.

Over the period 1980-2040, the assumption of equal growth rates of benefits and earnings leads to an average annual increase of 0.63 per cent in the financing burden in Canada and an increase of 0.70 in Germany. These are the amounts by which tax and contribution rates would have to be increased to finance the additional social expenditure arising from demographic change. By contrast, under the assumption that earnings grow 1.5 per cent faster per annum than benefits, the respective financing burdens *decrease* by 0.82 per cent and 0.74 per cent per annum. Each 0.5 percentage point increase in the assumed differential between benefit increases and earnings growth reduces the annual increase in the financing burden by an approximately equal amount, with a substantial impact on the cumulative change in the burden.

These examples serve to underline the point that the relationship between increases in real per capita social benefits and increases in productivity will have a major impact on the evolution of financing burdens. Slower growth of benefit levels relative to earnings would considerably ease the problem of coping with demographic pressures. Although past experience would suggest that it is unrealistic to assume that real benefit levels could be held substantially below real earnings over a long period of time, the relationship between the two is clearly an important policy issue in the context of population ageing.

For the purposes of the analysis so far, it has been assumed that labour force participation rates and unemployment rates remain constant over time. The future evolution of these factors is a matter of considerable uncertainty. Both will be subject to a range of influences, including demographic change. Obviously, an increase in labour force participation rates would counteract the shrinkage or slow growth of the working age population, thereby easing the problem of financing social programmes. In countries where unemployment rates are high at present, an improvement in labour market conditions would also free additional resources for coping with demographic pressures. And since the scope for holding real benefit increases below increases in real earnings over the longer term is likely to be limited, labour market developments will be particularly important in determining the capacity to finance social expenditures.

There are several groups which could potentially increase their labour force participation rates. These include workers age 55 and over, whose rates have declined significantly in recent decades, women, particularly married women, and young people in the 16-24

Table 25. **Projected growth of social expenditure, total earnings and financing burdens under alternative assumptions about the development of real benefits and real earnings**[a]**, 1980-2040**

	Average annual growth rate of real benefits per capita/real earnings per worker (%)[b]			
	3.0/3.0	3.0/3.5	3.0/4.0	3.0/4.5
	Average annual growth rate 1980-2040 (%):			
Canada				
Total real social expenditure[c]	4.08	4.08	4.08	4.08
Total real earnings[d]	3.43	3.94	4.44	4.94
Financing burden[e]	0.63	0.14	−0.34	−0.82
Cumulative increase in financing burden 1980-2040	45.76	8.76	−18.50	−38.88
Germany				
Total real social expenditure[c]	2.94	2.94	2.94	2.94
Total real earnings[d]	2.22	2.72	3.22	3.71
Financing burden[e]	0.70	0.21	−0.27	−0.74
Cumulative increase in financing burden 1980-2040	51.97	13.4	−15.0	−36.05

a) Based on medium fertility variant demographic assumptions.
b) First value in each pair is assumed annual percentage increase in real benefits per capita in each social programme. Second value is assumed annual percentage increase in real earnings per working-age person (15-64).
c) Product of projected increase in beneficiary population and assumed increase in real per capita benefits within each programme and age group.
d) Product of projected change in population aged 15-64 and assumed increase in real earnings per working-age person.
e) Yielded by c/d.
Source: OECD Secretariat estimates.

age group. Since participation rates of prime age males (25-44) are already very high there would appear to be little flexibility for further raising the rates among this group. A further potential source of labour force growth is migrant labour.

Slower growth or shrinkage of the working age population over the coming decades may lead to tighter labour market conditions and encourage increased participation among some or all of the above-mentioned groups, although it is difficult to estimate the size of the effect. The decline in the number of young people available to enter the labour force may create additional employment opportunities for women and older workers and could also lead to pressure to encourage immigration of labour. Thus, to the extent that the employment situation improves over the coming decades, it is likely that traditional labour market adjustment mechanisms will lead to some increase in participation by groups whose rates are currently below full potential.

There would also appear to be scope for policy interventions on several fronts. Participation rates of older workers will be particularly important in the context of the ageing of populations since they will affect both the number of workers available to finance social programmes and the number of elderly persons requiring support. Since declining participation among older workers is a rational response to employment problems on the one hand and improved pension provisions on the other hand, policy intervention may be warranted in both areas with a view to encouraging increased participation. Some countries may also choose, as in the past, to meet labour shortages by encouraging immigration of workers from less developed areas. These issues are taken up in Part III.

Assumptions Concerning Real Benefit Levels

As shown above, trends in real per capita benefit levels relative to average real earnings will be a key factor in determining how financing burdens evolve as the age structure of populations changes. As far as pension outlays are concerned, the schemes in a number of OECD countries are still some way short of maturity, implying a rise in real average benefit levels until such time as maturity is reached. In addition, there is likely to be considerable pressure to index benefits to earnings rather than prices so that relativity is maintained between wage-earners and the retired population. To the extent that such indexation is maintained, then some of the gains in real income made by the workforce will automatically be passed on to pensioners, leaving a smaller residual available for coping with the effects of demographic pressures. Policy measures which might be introduced to moderate the relative growth in pension expenditures include changing the indexation formula so that benefits do not fully keep pace with changes in average gross earnings, reducing the proportion of previous earnings replaced by the initial pension or raising the normal pensionable age.

A range of non-demographic factors will influence the pace at which health expenditure increases. Because of the labour intensive nature of health care services, per capita health care costs will tend to rise in line with general productivity over the longer term since there are likely to be strong pressures to maintain relativities between the earnings of health service workers and earnings elsewhere in the economy. In addition, advances in research and technology are likely to create strong pressures for additional spending on health care, potentially leading to increasing costs per patient. Costs for the elderly, who are major consumers of care, are particularly susceptible to the effects of technological developments. And in the absence of changes in age-related morbidity patterns, increasing life expectancy and the resultant rapid growth in the numbers of the very elderly may well magnify the demographic pressures on health care expenditure. Slower productivity growth in the health care sector than in the economy as a whole, which has been a feature of some health care systems in the past, would also push up real health care costs. Factors which might soften the cost impact of demographic change include reforms of health care financing and delivery systems, and improvements in the health status of the population through changes in lifestyle and behaviour. Some technological advances might also bring savings by enabling the replacement of expensive procedures by less costly forms of treatment. The critical question is whether economies emerging from these sources will be sufficient to offset the cost increases resulting from technological advances and other factors mentioned above.

In the case of education, teachers' salaries constitute the main expenditure item and here again pressure for the maintenance of relative earnings positions will tend to hold costs in line with general productivity in the economy. Moreover, a key assumption in the expenditure projections presented earlier is that education expenditure will contract in line with the projected decline in the school age population. It is questionable, however, whether it will prove feasible to reduce education expenditures by the amount suggested by demographic projections. On the demand side, pressure for improvements in the level of service, increased participation in non-compulsory education and the expansion of certain types of education, such as youth training programmes, will tend to push up average costs. On the supply side, potential savings are likely to be limited by diseconomies of scale and institutional rigidities, and it would be unrealistic to assume that attempts to reduce expenditures will not meet with political opposition.

NOTES AND REFERENCES

1. For Australia and the Netherlands, however, these expenditures are included. See Annex B for details.
2. See OECD, *Social Expenditure 1960-1990*, Paris, 1985.

SUMMARY OF PART II

In most of the countries considered in this analysis, with the exceptions of Japan and Germany, demographic developments do not give cause for concern before the early part of the next century. However, during the first quarter of the next century, changes in the age structure of populations will be particularly unfavourable for pension and health care systems and will add significantly to the burden of financing social programmes. Projection of current age-specific expenditure patterns indicates that demographic changes could add, on average, close to one per cent per annum to the financing burden borne by the working population. These prospective increases in the demographic pressure on social programmes appear unavoidable, resulting, as they do, largely from past changes in fertility.

Projected demographic changes also have important implications for the allocation of social expenditure among the various programmes and across the different age groups. Shifts in age structure imply a substantial diversion of resources from programmes serving the young to those serving the elderly. Even in the absence of pressure on the overall social budget, such shifts in resources are likely to pose managerial and political problems and to the extent that the resource shifts implied by demographic changes are not realised, the financial pressure on social programmes will be increased.

The consequences of the demographic changes will arise in the context of a growing economy, changing patterns of work, and retirement and social programmes which are still in the process of development. The evolution of economic and social systems cannot easily be foreseen, particularly in the long-term. However, given the demographic projections, it is necessary to consider what other key developments may exacerbate or ameliorate the pressures of population ageing, what scope exists in this context for policy measures, and when policy changes need to be put in place.

Several factors which will have an important impact on the development of social expenditure and the capacity to finance social programmes have been identified in Part II. The extent to which social expenditure can be restructured in response to changing patterns of demographic demand will have a substantial impact on the overall growth of expenditure. If increases in pension and health care costs for the elderly can be somewhat offset by reducing outlays on education and other programmes catering to the young, this would considerably reduce the growth of total social expenditure as the population ages. There will certainly be obstacles in the way of achieving such an offset and potential savings in outlays on the young should not be over-estimated, but this is an area which is subject to policy intervention. Trends in real per capita social benefits will also have an important impact on expenditure growth and the relationship between real benefit levels and real earnings of the working population will be a key factor in the evolution of the financing burden. Here again, there are influences which will tend to push up benefit levels but there is also considerable scope for policy intervention to moderate the growth of benefits. The capacity to finance increasing social outlays will depend largely on trends in productivity and the size of the employed population, factors which are themselves likely to be affected by the ageing of the working population. While productivity growth is likely to be only marginally amenable to policy intervention, the link between productivity and real benefit levels is open to manipulation, and there is also likely to be scope for influencing labour force participation rates of certain groups.

Policy measures which might help in coping with the effects of demographic changes are taken up in Part III. As far as the timing of policy changes is concerned, there is some degree of urgency even though the principal demographic effects are, with the exceptions of Japan and possibly Germany, still some way off. Early shifts in policy are needed because of the time required to change public commitments and individual behaviour. In most pension systems individual entitlements are built up over a working life and are embodied in formulae which frequently have the force of a legal contract. Commitments to education and health care systems are less explicit, but because they are based on a social consensus about what are the appropriate levels of benefit and entitlement they may also take some time to change. Similarly, adjustments of the labour market to encourage participation by older workers and changes in their expectations about the timing of their retirement are shifts which cannot occur quickly. Perhaps the most important conclusion of this part is that, for most countries, the increase in the elderly population, when it comes, will come quickly and it will be necessary to be prepared.

Part III

POLICY ISSUES AND CHOICES

INTRODUCTION

There are a number of areas where, on its present course, the evolution of social programmes appears likely to add to rather than subtract from the problems posed by demographic changes. This is the case in health care systems, where the control of health care expenditures and reform of financing are proving difficult, and where technological change and the care requirements of older patients will tend to push up costs in the future. It is also true of public pension systems generally, where it may be difficult to resist the demands that benefits be indexed to earnings. Especially vulnerable are those countries whose earnings-related pension systems will be maturing at the same time as their population structures are ageing. The key issue is whether, over the longer term, the growth of real per capita benefits in health care and pension systems can be held below the growth of average real earnings. In this context policy makers will have to address the question of how the distribution of resources between the working and retired population might be changed and what type of resource sharing between the two groups is appropriate in view of impending demographic changes. This relates not only to the level of benefits provided by social programmes but also to the financing base and the extent to which there may be scope for extending the tax base to include some sections of the elderly population.

There are several influences which might act to offset demographic pressures. In the first place, the resource requirements of education systems and other programmes targeting the young should grow more slowly than they have done in the past and, at least in terms of marginal increments, should be able to release resources for other social programmes. Such a switch in emphasis is, however, likely to pose managerial and political problems and may be limited in the case of education systems by institutional rigidities and diseconomies of scale. Sustained growth in productivity would ease the problem of coping with demographic pressures provided increases in real benefit levels do not absorb all the additional resources. The issue arises in this context, however, of how demographic change itself, particularly change in the age structure of the labour force, is likely to affect productivity. Increases in labour force participation rates would also ease the financing problem. Participation rates of older workers are particularly important since these affect both the support capacity of the working population and the demand on pension systems and other programmes serving the older population. There may be scope for increasing labour force participation rates of married women and younger people in some countries and the option of encouraging immigration of labour must also be considered. In this context the development of the employment situation and the feasibility and cost effectiveness of alternative methods of meeting labour shortages which may develop will be decisive factors.

Finally, the role of the private sector in providing social benefits and services must be considered. Private sector provision of income support and medical care is already substantial in some OECD countries and the expansion of such provision in the future could help to relieve some of the pressure on public social programmes. Private provision might also provide additional flexibility in responding to the varying needs of different age groups within the elderly population. The consequences for efficiency and effectiveness of changing the public-private mix would need to be examined carefully, as would the impact on distributional equity. It is important to note that irrespective of whether social benefits are provided through public or private programmes, the changing age structure will still require a substantial increase in the share of national resources channelled to the elderly population.

The first chapter of this part addresses the question of restructuring social expenditure in response to demographic shifts. It examines the potential for achieving savings on family benefits and education, and the shift in resources within the health care system from areas such as child health services and acute care to areas such as long-term care for the elderly. The second chapter discusses the impact which population ageing is likely to have on productivity and labour force growth and what scope there may be for policy intervention to boost the capacity to finance social programmes. The final two chapters examine the two policy areas which will be most closely affected by the ageing of populations, health care and pensions. Factors likely to influence the growth of expenditure in these areas are discussed and some of the major policy issues are explored.

Chapter 6

RESTRUCTURING SOCIAL EXPENDITURE

As shown in Part II, the extent to which changing demographic structures can be used as a basis for restructuring social expenditure will have an important impact on the growth of total social expenditure as the population ages. If public social outlays for the young were to vary exactly in line with projected numbers of young people, this would provide a considerable, although not total, offset against increasing outlays for the elderly and would relieve some of the pressure of financing social programmes.

Of the countries for which expenditure projections have been made, the potential for reducing outlays on the young is greatest in European countries and in Japan, where the number of children is actually projected to fall over the coming decades. In Australia, Canada and the United States the child population is projected to grow over the projection period as a whole, but some shrinkage is projected in the North American countries in the first decade of the next century, while in Australia the number of children is projected to remain virtually constant during this period. Thus, in these countries also there should be potential for some saving on programmes catering to the young.

There are, however, good reasons to suppose that expenditure on education and other programmes catering for the young will not contract to the extent indicated by demographic developments. Certain inherent characteristics of the programmes in question are likely to increase real costs per beneficiary and the achievement of even quite small savings will require considerable political effort and institutional flexibility.

Family Benefits

Flexibility for adjusting expenditure in line with changing beneficiary numbers is likely to be greatest in the case of cash transfers. Provided average real benefits were held constant, expenditure on family benefits would automatically vary according to changes in the number of recipients. And since coverage of family benefit programmes is universal or near-universal in most OECD countries, there is little scope for cost increases due to extensions of coverage. There are, however, several sources of potential pressure to increase

average real per capita benefits, which would reduce savings on child benefit programmes.

The proportion of single-parent families is rising in many OECD countries. Since such families generally receive larger benefits due to their higher vulnerability to poverty, their increasing weight within the beneficiary population can be expected to raise average benefit levels. The incidence of child poverty has also risen in a number of countries in recent years and the living standards of families with children have, on average, deteriorated relative to other groups, including the elderly. Consequently, there could be considerable pressure to increase the benefits provided to low income families. Moreover, if the living standards of other groups in society are rising it may not be politically feasible to hold family benefits constant in real terms.

Some countries channel considerable assistance to families through tax relief in respect of dependent children. Such tax expenditures have not been included in the projections in Part II. Slower growth or shrinkage of the child population should reduce the scale of tax expenditures, thus freeing resources which could theoretically be used for other purposes.

In general, however, expenditure on family benefits, whether in the form of cash transfers or tax relief, represents a very small portion of total social expenditure. Even in the event that savings could be achieved in this area, the amount of resources freed would be tiny compared to outlays on health and pensions, and therefore would have only a minor impact on the overall growth of social expenditure.

Health Care

Shrinkage or slower growth of the young population will also enable some saving on child health care expenditure, although, as noted in Part II, per capita public outlays on health services are much higher for the elderly than for the young. As children are not heavy users of hospital based services, the potential for realising savings in this area is likely to be insignificant. Falling fertility rates will reduce the use of maternity hospital facilities, although the effect on total expenditure for hospital services is not large. With regard to community-based care, the main potential for saving

51

will be in areas such as school health services, immunisation programmes and home health visitor services for children. Projected shrinkage in the younger adult age groups (15-44) in many countries should also provide some potential for saving on community-based health services used by these age groups, although this effect will be far outweighed by the increasing demands of growing elderly populations.

Whether savings on younger age groups can be used to provide a partial offset to increasing outlays on services for the elderly, will depend on the extent to which health care facilities and staffing levels are adjusted to changing patterns of demand. Overall, however, the growth of health care costs is likely to be determined less by demographic factors than by decisions regarding the delivery and financing of care. In particular, increases in the numbers of very elderly persons are likely to put considerable pressure on chronic and long-term care facilities. The institutional setting in which such care is provided and the extent to which its expansion is counterbalanced by shifting resources out of acute care facilities will have a major impact on expenditure growth. These issues are taken up in Chapter 8.

Education

The largest public outlays on behalf of the young are in the area of education. In 1981 education absorbed, on average, almost 23 per cent of the total social budget in OECD countries, although there is considerable cross-national variation in the share[1]. As shown in Part II, savings on education could have a major impact on the overall growth of social expenditure as populations age. Under the medium fertility variant population projections, and assuming no change in real per capita costs per pupil, education expenditure would fall in most of the countries examined. Expenditures would remain static in Canada and the United States over the projection period as a whole and they would rise in Australia (see Table 19).

In the past, however, demographic trends have proved a poor guide to the growth of education expenditure. Since 1960 expenditure has grown much more rapidly than the school age population, and although growth rates have declined in recent years, expenditure has not contracted to the same extent as the numbers of school age children[1]. The main causes of rising expenditure in the past have been increases in the average real cost per pupil and relative price increases in the education sector[2]. In view of experience over the past several decades, the projections presented in Part II may greatly over-estimate the potential for saving on education costs.

Future expenditure trends will depend to some extent on whether school enrolments vary in line with the school age population. Enrolments in the compulsory level of the school system can be expected to follow trends in the relevant age groups, but there may be potential for increased demand at both the pre-compulsory and post-compulsory levels which could push up enrolment rates and thus increase costs.

In 1980, enrolment rates at pre-compulsory level were well below 50 per cent of the relevant age groups in almost two-thirds of OECD countries[1]. There is, therefore, considerable potential for increased demand. Such demand could well arise due to factors such as rising employment rates among mothers of young children and growth in the number of single-parent families. Whether increased demand will actually be met by expansion of public provision is a matter for policy makers to decide, but in the event that enrolments are allowed to expand, savings due to demographic change will be reduced.

Enrolment rates at post-compulsory level vary quite considerably between countries, but in most cases there would appear to be potential for further expansion[1]. Enrolments at this level are sensitive to a range of influences other than demographic change. Secular increases in real household income and educational level of parents are likely to lead to rising participation rates among their children, while increases in the likelihood of life-long labour force attachment for women and improvement in their earnings prospects, which enhance the potential returns from continuing education, may encourage a higher proportion of young women to stay on at school[3]. Post-compulsory participation rates are also sensitive to cyclical factors such as unemployment rates and relative earnings levels of less and better educated school leavers[1,4].

Aside from possible increases in participation rates of the traditional school and college age groups, there will be demands on education systems from new groups. Non-formal education and training has become an increasingly important element in the post-compulsory education system in recent years and its importance may well increase in the future as a result of new industrial training needs. Rising unemployment in recent years has also prompted the development of a range of public training and re-training programmes, particularly for unemployed school leavers. While the need for such programmes may decline if the employment situation improves, they are unlikely to disappear entirely. Changing skill requirements in the employment market and the difficulty of rapid adaptation of the formal curriculum are likely to prompt a continuing need for informal training programmes.

Another potentially important source of expansion is the increasing demand for adult education. Periods of retraining over the working life are likely to take on greater importance in the coming decades due to ageing of the workforce and the rapid pace of technological change. Increased demand is also likely to come from the elderly, as successive generations of retirees live longer, retire in good health and have a higher level of basic education. Thus, it is quite possible that shrinkage of the school age population will be offset by increasing enrolment rates and the emergence of new demands on the education system.

Even in a situation of falling enrolments the realisation of savings is likely to prove difficult. Teachers' salaries represent the major element in education expenditure and to the extent that the teaching profession succeeds in maintaining wage relativities with workers in the private sector, the cost per pupil can be expected to rise at the same rate as productivity. Salaries of teachers and other public service workers have been held down in some countries in recent years, but usually at the cost of vigorous protest and disruption of services. It is unlikely that such a policy could be sustained over a long period. Thus, while there may be some slippage in relative salary levels, it is unreasonable to expect that real salary increases for teachers could be held much below those for other workers over the longer term. And if, as has happened in the past, productivity in the education sector were to lag behind general productivity, this would further increase the real cost per pupil.

It may also prove difficult to hold teacher/pupil ratios constant in the context of falling enrolments. Staffing levels are affected by diseconomies of scale and since teachers in most OECD countries hold tenured positions, reductions in staff numbers have to be obtained through natural wastage rather than redundancies. In countries where the teaching profession is strongly unionised it may prove particularly difficult to adjust staffing levels. Thus, staff levels may be adjusted to changing enrolment levels only after a considerable time lag. A further constraint arises from the fact that shrinkage of the school age population will affect different levels of the school system at different times and there may also be regional discontinuities in the rate of change. Since the capacity for redeploying teaching staff from one level of the system to another and across regions is likely to be limited, it is improbable that staffing levels will be reduced to the extent suggested by aggregate enrolment changes.

Capital investment in school buildings and equipment is also unlikely to fall in line with enrolments. Apart from the diseconomies of scale due to geographical variations in enrolment trends mentioned above, the political difficulties of closing and amalgamating schools will limit the scope for rationalisation. Moreover, costs for maintenance and services such as heating are unlikely to fall pro rata with pupil numbers. And since many countries reduced capital outlays on education in the second half of the 1970s or early 1980s, there is likely to be a backlog of needs which will require additional expenditure in the coming years. Finally, the quality of education has emerged as an important issue in recent years and there may, therefore, be pressures to use the opportunity of falling pupil numbers to increase outlays per pupil.

Even in the event that savings on education are achieved, there may be obstacles to using the resulting resources to finance programmes for the elderly. In the first place, the projections indicate that the main potential for reducing outlays on the young occurs between now and the early part of the next century. Under the medium variant fertility assumption, the young population stabilises in many countries in the second decade of the next century and begins to increase gradually thereafter. Within this scenario the potential for saving on programmes for the young would largely have passed by the time expenditures on the elderly begin to increase rapidly. In the event of continuing low fertility there would, of course, be potential for further contraction of the school system. Nevertheless, it is uncertain whether any significant savings on education will be possible during the period when population ageing will be placing most pressure on health care and pension expenditures.

A second potential obstacle in the way of using savings on education to finance increases in the cost of other social programmes is that in some OECD countries educational services are controlled by provincial or state authorities and funded largely from local taxation, whereas pension and health care systems tend to be centrally controlled and funded. As such, there is no guarantee that if and when education expenditures decrease, local authorities will be willing to either reduce tax levels, thus facilitating an increase in central taxation to fund programmes for the elderly, or to undertake part of the financing of these programmes. Such efforts to redeploy resources between programmes could generate considerable political tension.

The issues raised here serve to highlight the fact that expenditure projections made on the basis of demographic developments alone provide an over-optimistic picture concerning the savings which can be made on education and other programmes catering to the young. The savings which can actually be realised are likely to be considerably less than the corresponding change in population numbers and to provide a much more limited offset to increasing expenditure on the elderly than indicated by the projections in Part II.

Chapter 7

THE IMPACT OF POPULATION AGEING ON PRODUCTIVITY AND THE LABOUR FORCE

Concern over the capacity to finance projected increases in social expenditure is at the centre of the debate over the social policy implications of population ageing. Future trends in labour force growth and productivity will be crucial in determining the increases in tax and contribution rates necessary to finance additional social expenditure. However, these economic variables may themselves be affected by changes in the age structure of the population.

Population Ageing and Productivity

As shown in Chapter 2, the working age-population in OECD countries is growing progressively older. By the second decade of the next century it is projected that the proportion of the potential workforce in the young (15-24) and prime (25-44) age groups will have fallen considerably, while the proportion aged 45 and over will have risen correspondingly. Unfortunately, there is little empirical evidence concerning the possible effects of such changes in age structure on labour force productivity.

Studies of individual productivity indicate that the effect of age is relatively marginal and that productivity variations within age groups are more significant than variations across age groups[5]. To the extent, however, that productvity improves over the working life due to accumulated experience and skill, the ageing of the labour force might be expected to boost productivity. The effect would also depend on how closely age-earning profiles reflected age-productivity profiles. Since the value of accumulated experience is, however, likely to be diminished by rapid technological change, provision for retraining older workers could become an important element in the maintenance of productivity. This is an area where policy intervention is likely to be necessary.

It is generally thought that the mobility of workers declines with age[6]. To the extent that older workers are less willing or able than younger ones to shift between occupations, industries or geographical areas, ageing of the labour force could lead to loss of efficiency in the allocation of labour. If this were to cause difficulties in adjusting to changing patterns of consumer demand, technological innovation or foreign competition, there could be a detrimental effect on economic growth[7].

The maintenance or enhancement of flexibility as the labour force ages is, however, open to policy intervention on several fronts. Factors such as access to retraining, portability of pension rights and the extent of age discrimination in job offers are all likely to affect the mobility of older workers. The availability of unemployment, disability or early retirement benefits as compared with the costs of changing jobs is also likely to be influential[8].

An important determinant of future productivity growth will be the amount of capital available per worker. With slower growth or shrinkage of the labour force in the coming decades, the capital/worker ratio might be expected to rise, thus offsetting some of the above-mentioned effects of an ageing labour force. Indeed it has been suggested that changes in age structure might increase the growth of capital through effects on the household saving rate[9]. Life-cycle models indicate that household saving is typically highest between middle age and retirement. As such, the aggregate rate of saving might be expected to increase as the proportion of older workers rises over the next several decades. However, this effect would presumably be offset after the turn of the century by growth in the proportion of persons over retirement age, who typically save less or draw on savings. It must be pointed out that attempts to simulate the effect of a changing age structure on the aggregate rate of saving have not produced conclusive results[10]. Moreover, even if a clear relationship between age structure and the rate of saving could be established, it is by no means certain that this relationship would hold true for the future.

While the future growth of productivity would appear to be only marginally influenced by policy intervention, the impact of such growth on the social expenditure financing burden may be more amenable to manipulation. As indicated by the projections in Part II, the relationship between real per capita benefit rates and productivity changes will be crucial in determining the financing burden, whatever the rate of productivity growth. In the case of education, the discussion in Chapter 6 suggests that that labour-intensive nature of education will render it difficult to hold the cost per pupil much below general productivity growth over the longer term. Institutional rigidities and diseconomies of scale could further increase per capita costs as the school age population declines. Per capita costs in health care systems have outstripped productivity gains in many countries in the past and, for reasons which are discussed later in this part, the prospects for holding costs down in the future should not be overestimated. The relationship between pension rates and productivity depends on how the initial benefit is related to past earnings and how benefits are indexed. Prospects for adjusting this relationship in order to curb the growth of pension expenditure are also taken up below. However, the feasibility of holding increases in per capita benefit levels much below increases in average real earnings over the long term is questionable.

Labour Force Prospects

In view of the fact that the capacity to alter the relationship between productivity growth and per capita social benefit levels will probably be quite limited, coping with the costs of population ageing is likely to depend to a large extent on labour force trends. In short, the more workers there are the less the social dependency burden will increase. This statement is subject to the qualification that it is the level of employment and not merely the size of the labour force which determines the dependency burden. The high unemployment rates of recent years in many OECD countries have added considerably to the problem of financing social programmes. Thus, whatever the trend in labour force growth, a return to low levels of unemployment would ease the financing problem. Moreover, unemployment rates are likely to influence labour force participation rates for some groups, including teenagers, women and older workers[11].

As shown in Chapter 2, growth of the working-age population has begun to decelerate in many OECD countries as a result of reductions in the size of young cohorts now reaching working age. The downturn in fertility rates since the mid-1960s will lead to further tapering off in growth rates over the remainder of this century and it is projected that by the second decade of the next century almost all countries will be experiencing shrinkage of the working-age population.

However, demographic trends provide only a partial guide to prospective changes in the size and structure of the labour force. Future developments in labour force

Table 26. **Aggregate labour force participation rates**[a]

Percentages

	Total		Male		Female		Female/Male[k]	
	1965	1984	1965	1984	1965	1984	1965	1984
Australia	67.7	69.9	94.1	85.6	40.0	52.7	42.5	61.6
Austria	67.7[b]	67.3	87.2[b]	79.9	50.1[b]	55.2	57.5	69.1
Belgium	63.0	63.9	88.2	77.8[g]	38.0	49.6[g]	43.1	63.8
Canada	63.9[c]	72.8	88.0[c]	84.5	39.7[c]	61.2	45.1	72.4
Denmark	73.0	81.7	96.8	87.6[g]	49.3	74.2[g]	50.9	84.7
Finland	74.7	78.3	87.6	82.7	62.6	74.0	71.5	89.5
France	67.2	66.0	89.7	77.4	45.7	54.7	50.9	70.7
Germany	70.5	64.3	94.1	79.3	49.0	49.4	52.1	62.3
Ireland	67.3	62.6	98.7	87.1[g]	35.2	37.9[g]	35.7	43.5
Italy	61.8	60.1	90.5	79.7	34.6	41.1	38.2	51.6
Japan	71.9	72.7	88.6	88.3	55.8	57.2	63.0	64.8
Netherlands	59.3[d]	59.5	76.0[c]	80.1[g]	25.8[e]	39.8[g]	33.9	49.7
New Zealand	63.7	65.2	92.5	84.6[g]	34.2	45.8[g]	37.0	54.1
Norway	63.5	76.3	89.9	86.3	36.9	66.1	41.0	76.6
Portugal[f]	61.2	65.6	103.3	84.0[g]	23.6	53.2[g]	22.8	63.3
Spain	61.5	55.5	96.4[d]	78.6	29.2[d]	32.7	30.3	41.6
Sweden	72.9	81.5	91.4	85.5	54.1	77.4	59.2	90.5
Switzerland[h]	78.6	68.7	106.5	89.9[g]	51.6	48.8[g]	48.5	54.3
United Kingdom	72.8	73.3	97.1	87.6	49.0	59.0	50.5	67.4
United States	66.2	73.4	88.7	84.9	44.3	62.8	49.9	74.0

a) (Labour force/population aged 15 to 64 years) × 100.
b) 1968.
c) 1966.
d) 1970.
e) 1971.
f) Labour force data include a number of persons aged less than 15 years and 65 years and over.
g) 1983.
h) Population data exclude a number of foreign and seasonal workers who are included in the labour force estimates.
k) Female participation rate as a percentage of male participation rate.
Source: OECD, *Labour Force Statistics*, various years.

Table 27. **Participation trends by age group in selected countries**

Percentages[a]

	Males				Females			
	15 - 24	25 - 54	55 - 64	65 +	15 - 24	25 - 54	55 - 64	65 +
Australia								
1965[b]	78.9	97.3	85.8	23.3	60.8	37.3	21.0	4.4
1970	76.5	97.2	85.1	22.1	59.7	43.4	23.3	3.7
1975	74.7	95.9	78.8	16.7	61.2	49.6	23.7	3.9
1980	76.4	94.5	68.8	11.1	65.1	53.3	22.0	2.9
1985	73.7	93.5	60.4	8.9	65.0	57.2	19.3	2.0
Canada								
1965	57.2	97.1	86.4	26.3	39.0	33.9	27.0	6.0
1970	61.8	96.2	84.2	22.6	46.3	39.8	29.8	5.0
1975	68.8	94.8	79.4	18.5	56.8	50.5	30.8	5.0
1980	72.0	94.8	76.2	14.7	62.6	60.1	33.7	4.3
1985	70.1	93.8	70.2	12.3	64.6	68.2	33.8	4.2
Finland								
1965	65.8	94.8	81.5	18.0	54.7	67.9	54.9	3.8
1970	58.0	93.4	71.1	19.0	51.5	70.2	46.3	4.4
1975	51.3	91.6	62.1	10.3	48.9	78.0	44.4	2.8
1980	57.1	93.3	57.3	17.0	52.0	83.0	43.0	6.0
1985	62.6	93.5	57.8	10.6	54.9	86.7	52.9	4.8
France								
1965	65.3	96.1	76.0	28.3	49.8	42.8	36.9	11.5
1970	60.3	96.8	75.4	19.5	47.2	50.1	40.0	8.6
1975	55.6	96.4	68.9	13.9	45.6	57.3	35.9	5.8
1980	52.5	96.4	68.5	7.5	43.2	63.0	39.7	3.3
1985	49.0	95.9	50.1	5.3	40.3	68.9	31.0	2.2
Germany								
1965	78.1	96.6	84.6	24.0	69.3	46.1	30.2	7.8
1970	71.6	97.1	82.2	19.9	61.9	47.6	29.9	6.5
1975	66.4	95.1	68.1	10.8	58.6	51.6	24.8	4.5
1980	62.2	93.6	65.5	7.0	53.4	53.6	27.2	3.1
1985	60.5	91.4	57.5	5.2	53.5	56.4	23.9	2.5
Italy	[c]	[d]	[e]	[c]	[d]	[e]		
1965	60.9	94.7	54.8	18.4	39.3	28.8	14.3	4.7
1970	52.1	93.9	48.2	12.9	35.5	28.3	10.6	2.6
1975	44.8	94.0	42.4	10.4	31.6	31.3	8.5	2.1
1980	49.4	93.1	39.6	12.6	41.2	39.9	11.0	3.5
1985[f]	48.1	92.1	38.2	8.9	40.7	43.8	10.5	2.1
Japan								
1965	59.0	96.7	86.7	56.3	51.8	56.0	45.3	21.6
1970	57.7	97.3	86.6	49.4	53.4	55.1	44.4	17.9
1975	50.2	97.4	86.0	44.4	45.6	52.3	43.7	15.3
1980	42.9	97.0	85.4	41.0	43.9	56.7	45.3	15.5
1985	42.6	96.7	83.0	37.0	43.2	60.3	45.3	15.5
Netherlands								
1965	..	..	..	..	..	..	..	..
1970[g]	64.8	96.4	80.8	11.4	53.0	23.1	14.9	2.3
1975	55.1	95.1	73.0	8.0	49.1	28.7	14.3	1.8
1980	49.7	93.6	63.6	4.8	47.6	37.2	14.3	0.9
1985	48.6	93.3	53.8	4.0	48.8	46.8	14.5	0.7
Spain	[j]				[j]			
1965	..	..	..	..	..	..	..	..
1970[h]	70.6	96.5	84.2	25.9	47.7	25.1	22.0	7.7
1975	68.6	96.5	79.8	18.8	49.0	27.9	23.0	6.3
1980	69.4	94.8	75.7	12.3	47.9	30.6	21.2	3.8
1985	64.4	94.1	66.3	5.9	44.2	35.5	20.0	2.1

56

Table 27. *(cont'd)*

	Males				Females			
	15 - 24	25 - 54	55 - 64	65 +	15 - 24	25 - 54	55 - 64	65 +
Sweden	*j*				*j*			
1965	71.7	96.2	88.3	37.7	60.5	56.0	39.2	11.6
1970	67.0	94.8	85.4	28.9	59.4	64.2	44.5	8.7
1975	72.4	95.2	82.0	19.9	66.2	74.3	49.6	6.1
1980	71.5	95.4	78.7	14.2	70.1	82.9	55.3	3.7
1985	65.7	95.2	76.0	11.0	66.4	88.9	59.9	3.2
United Kingdom	*j*				*j*			
1965	77.4	98.4	92.7	23.7	61.0	48.1	35.6	6.5
1970	74.7	97.8	91.3	20.2	56.7	53.2	39.3	6.4
1975	67.9	96.1	87.8	15.8	56.4	61.3	40.3	4.9
1980	70.5	96.1	81.8	10.5	62.2	64.0	39.2	3.6
1985	71.6	95.2	66.4	7.6	63.1	67.0	34.1	3.2
United States	*j*				*j*			
1965	70.9	95.7	82.9	26.6	43.6	45.1	40.3	9.4
1970	71.8	94.8	80.7	25.7	50.7	49.7	42.2	9.0
1975	73.2	93.8	74.6	20.7	57.1	55.0	40.7	7.8
1980	74.5	93.4	71.2	18.3	61.7	63.8	41.0	7.6
1985	75.3	90.8	59.7	10.3	63.7	69.5	41.7	6.8

a) The participation rate for a given age group is defined as the ratio between the total civilian labour force for the age group divided by the population for the age group.
b) 1966; *c)* 14-24; *d)* 25-59; *e)* 60-64; *f)* 1984; *g)* 1971; *h)* 1972; *j)* 16-24.
Source: OECD, *Labour Force Statistics*, Paris, 1985, 1986.

participation rates by age and sex will be a key factor influencing labour force growth. The crucial question in the context of this study is whether there is any prospect of an increase in aggregate participation rates which could offset the shrinkage of the working-age population and thus alleviate the problem of financing social programmes in the first half of the next century.

Some clues to future prospects may be provided by past trends. As shown in Table 26, trends in aggregate participation rates in OECD countries have varied considerably over the past two decades. Participation has declined in Germany, Ireland and Spain, has remained virtually stable in Australia, Japan and the United Kingdom, and has increased significantly in other countries. These patterns are the outcome of two opposing developments: there has been a decline in male participation rates across all OECD countries, and a rise in female participation rates.

Table 27 provides a more detailed account of participation rate changes in selected OECD countries since the mid-1960s. While rates of participation vary across countries, trends have been very similar. In all countries participation rates for males aged 65 and over have declined markedly and rates for males in the 55-64 age group have also declined quite significantly. Participation rates for prime age males (25-54) have remained relatively stable, while those for young men have declined in European countries and in Japan, but have risen in North America. Female participation rates have behaved quite differently. Large increases have been recorded in participation by prime age females and participation by females in the 55-64 age group has also

risen in several countries, albeit less dramatically. In most cases, however, participation by females in this age group has declined slightly or remained stable. Participation by females aged 65 and over has declined everywhere except Finland, but the decline has been much less sharp than in the case of males. Participation by females in the 15-24 age group has risen in North America, Australia, Sweden and the United Kingdom, has remained virtually stable in Finland, Italy and Spain, and has declined elsewhere.

Since participation rates for prime age males are already high, the main potential for increasing participation concerns young people, women and older males. Encouragement of immigration by foreign workers would also swell the ranks of the labour force. Employment prospects for all of these groups will obviously depend on the level and structure of labour demand in the coming decades, something which is difficult to predict. Given that the working-age population will continue to expand in many countries up to the end of the century, albeit at a reduced rate, and in view of the persistence of high unemployment rates in many European countries, substantial employment creation will be required simply to absorb the increasing numbers of working age people and to reduce unemployment rates. Thus the opportunity for increasing participation rates may be limited during this period. Exceptions to this pattern include Germany, Italy, Japan, Austria, Belgium, Denmark and Switzerland, where the working-age population should begin to shrink in the 1990s. After the turn of the century, reduced growth or shrinkage of the working-age population in an increasing number of countries could lead to labour shortages, thus improving employment opportunities and encouraging increased labour force participation. This will, of course, depend on trends in the demand for labour.

Migrant Workers

Encouragement of immigration by foreign workers has provided a partial solution to shortages in domestic labour supply in the past in a number of OECD countries and some countries may choose to adopt such a policy again in the future. But quite apart from the fact that the influx of immigrant workers would need to be very large to fully compensate for shrinkage of the working-age population in many European countries, such a solution is not cost free[12]. The integration of foreign workers, who are usually drawn predominantly from less developed regions, is likely to require expensive training, resettlement, and social policy measures for the workers and their families. And while foreign workers initially swell the ranks of those contributing to social security systems, by so doing they acquire benefit entitlements and so eventually increase the beneficiary population also. There may also be social and political barriers to encouraging large scale immigration. In all, the viability of such a policy should not be over-estimated; at best it may provide a very partial solution to the problem of declining working-age populations.

Prospects for Labour Supply of Youth and Women

Falling youth labour force participation rates over the past several decades are attributable in large part to increasing participation in post-compulsory education. However, participation rates of teenagers are also sensitive to the state of the labour market and the high youth unemployment rates of recent years have encouraged young people to stay on longer in school in order to improve their employment prospects[13]. Now that the numbers of young people are beginning to decline, employment prospects for youth may improve, possibly inducing an increase in labour force participation rates. But even in the event of a return to the youth participation rates experienced in 1979, before the latest upturn in youth unemployment, many countries would still be affected by a decline in the number of entry level workers and in the overall size of the working population in the early decades of the next century.

Over the past two decades the labour force participation rates of women have increased significantly in the majority of OECD countries. However, as may be seen from Table 26, the rates still vary considerably from one country to another. Whereas the ratio of the female participation rate to the male rate was between 85 and 90 per cent in some of the Scandinavian countries in 1984, it was as low as 42 to 43 per cent in Ireland and Spain. The average ratio for the OECD area in 1984 was

67 per cent. There may be considerable potential for growth of the female labour force if the ratios currently prevailing in the Scandinavian countries could be approached in other countries.

Trends in real wage rates for women and in the demand for female labour are likely to exercise a major influence on participation in the future. Further narrowing of wage differentials between men and women, as well as moves towards equal treatment of the sexes in matters of social security and taxation can be expected to encourage participation by increasing the economic incentives to take paid employment. Additional growth of opportunities for part-time employment, further expansion of the service sector, and movement of women into newly emerging areas of employment and into traditionally male occupations would also facilitate increased participation. The effect of these factors will be mitigated by the level of unemployment and by fertility trends, although variations in these are unlikely to exert a major influence on the underlying upward trend in participation.

It is essential to note, however, that growth in female employment is unlikely to provide a one-for-one offset for the decline in male participation in terms of replacement of the tax base. A large proportion of female participation is in part-time employment and the proportion has risen substantially in most countries over the period since 1973. As a result of the concentration of women in part-time employment, and due also to persisting differentials between average earnings for male and female workers in full-time occupations, the average earnings of women are appreciably lower than those of men. Therefore, although the number of women entering the labour force has more than compensated for the number of older men withdrawing, this has not been equivalent to a replacement of the tax base. In view of the continuing structural shift to services, which favours the expansion of part-time employment, and given that part-time workers are increasingly favoured by employers as a way of achieving greater work force flexibility, it is likely that a large proportion of female employment will continue to be part-time in the medium term.

Labour Supply of Older Workers

Even in the event of further growth in youth and female labour force participation rates, trends in participation by older workers are likely to be an important determinant of the capacity to finance increases in the cost of social programmes. A continuation or intensification of the current trend of declining participation by workers aged 55 and over would not only subtract from the labour force but would add appreciably to the cost of social security programmes. Conversely, an increase in participation rates of older workers would provide an important offset to the cost of providing for growing numbers of elderly and very elderly since the number of contributors to social security schemes would be increased by those staying on in work, while the number drawing benefits would be decreased.

Apart from the financial considerations, an increase in the age of withdrawal from the labour force might also be justified on the grounds of increasing life expectancy. Retirees are, on average, now living for several years longer than when current retirement age norms were originally established. Further projected improvements in life expectancy imply that with a static retirement age, future retirees will be drawing benefits for longer than is the case today. Thus, an increase in the retirement age could be viewed simply as an adjustment to the changing life span. And to the extent that increases in life expectancy reflect improvements in the health status of older age groups, an increasing proportion of older persons may be able and willing to remain in the labour force.

There are two elements to the decrease in labour force participation rates of older male workers. As may be seen from Table 27, participation rates of men above normal retirement age (65 in most countries) have fallen steadily, although the rates vary between countries. There has also been a marked fall in participation rates of older men below normal retirement age in many countries. Participation rates of older women have generally been more stable, although it may be the case that older women have been discouraged from entering the labour market in recent years due to high unemployment.

A variety of explanations have been suggested for the secular decline in participation rates of older workers, including improvements in pension provisions, changes in labour market conditions, increasing preference for leisure and changes in socio-economic characteristics of successive cohorts. Such characteristics might include health status, social class, occupation, marital status and wives' labour force status. Empirical research in a number of countries indicates that among the above factors, developments in pension provisions and labour market conditions have been particularly influential in encouraging earlier withdrawal from the labour force[14].

With respect to pension provisions, developments such as expanded coverage of public and private schemes, increases in earnings-replacement ratios of benefits, relaxation of earnings tests and, in a few cases, reductions in the normal retirement age have all increased the economic incentives for withdrawal from the labour force on either a full-time or part-time basis. Withdrawal from the labour force before normal retirement age has been facilitated in many countries by the introduction of a variety of early retirement provisions, particularly since the mid-1970s when labour market conditions began to deteriorate. Such provisions include early pensions for long-term unemployed older workers, easier access to disability pensions, actuarially reduced pensions several years before the normal retirement age and special early retirement schemes. Available data on the take-up of early retirement provisions indicate that they have proved attractive to older workers, although it is unclear to what extent they may have increased the rate of withdrawal from the workforce.

Participation rates of older workers may also be sensitive to the level of unemployment in the economy. Unemployment rates among older males are higher than the rates among prime age males in many OECD countries, although the rates for older females are lower than those for prime age female workers in most countries[15]. And while it has proved difficult to measure the extent to which unemployment among older workers is obscured by early retirement due to discouragement, evidence from the United States and Australia suggests that discouragement may be a serious problem[16].

One reason for the higher incidence of discouragement among older workers may be that when such workers become unemployed, they face the longest average duration of unemployment of any age group. This is clearly illustrated by the data on the incidence of long-term (12 months and over) unemployment shown in Table 28. In 1985, over 80 per cent of unemployed older workers in Belgium and over two-thirds in Finland, France, and the Netherlands were out of work for 12 months or more. Among the countries shown here, the incidence of long-term unemployment among older workers was, on average, five times higher than among youths and one-and-a-half times higher than among prime age adults.

Future employment prospects for older workers will depend partly on trends in the aggregate demand for labour. In the shorter term, the persistence of high levels of unemployment in a number of OECD countries is likely to limit demand, and hence the jobs available for older workers. In the longer term, however, there may be a possibility of increasing demand for older workers as the inflow of younger workers declines. Such labour shortages as do occur are likely to be concentrated in entry-level jobs. Whether such jobs can be filled by older workers will depend on the substitutability and complementarity existing among different groups in the labour force. Mismatches between supply and demand may arise if older workers are unable to fill entry-level jobs due to inappropriate skills or lack of mobility, or are unwilling to do so because of the cuts in wage levels this would imply under the current age structure of earnings.

Labour market mismatches are likely to be partially resolved through traditional labour market adjustment mechanisms. With a shrinking labour force, employers will have incentives to encourage participation by older workers. Indeed there are some indications that shortages of entry-level workers in parts of the United States are already prompting employers to hire older people[17]. However, policies to increase the attractiveness to employers of older workers and to encourage such workers to remain in the labour force are also likely to be required. In this context measures to retrain older workers, to facilitate occupational mobility, to promote

Table 28. The incidence of long-term unemployment
by age and sex

Percentage of long-term unemployment in total unemployment
within age and sex groups

	Year	Youths	Prime-age adults	Older workers	Males	Females
Australia	1979	15.3	17.2	33.0	19.3	16.7
	1982	14.2	19.6	36.2	19.4	18.4
	1985	22.9	31.2	53.9	36.6	22.0
Austria	1979	3.1	7.8	20.1	12.0	6.5
	1982	1.9	5.6	16.2	6.1	5.2
	1985	5.3	16.7	30.4	16.4	10.0
Belgium	1979	39.4	62.0	73.8	46.6	64.5
	1982	42.6	64.2	74.4	49.9	67.4
	1984	50.0	72.1	81.7	63.4	72.0
Canada	1979	2.4	4.4	4.6	4.1	2.7
	1982	4.0	5.7	7.8	5.9	4.5
	1985	5.2	11.3	18.2	12.1	8.0
Finland	1980	6.3	26.8	51.9	25.5	28.3
	1982	10.0	28.8	50.0	26.4	34.7
	1984	3.3	22.9	72.6	33.3	42.9
France	1979	21.1	31.7	49.8	26.4	33.2
	1982	36.6	39.8	61.0	35.1	48.0
	1985	37.5	48.8	67.2	42.7	50.5
Germany	1979	6.8	16.6	34.9	22.2	18.1
	1982	10.4	21.2	34.5	20.9	21.7
	1984	15.9	33.8	47.4	34.2	31.0
Ireland	1980	18.8	34.0	48.6	38.8	22.3
	1982	17.2	33.1	46.1	35.3	20.5
	1985	27.5	44.4	52.4	45.0	29.9
Japan	1979	5.9	20.0	20.0	18.4	13.5
	1982	7.1	16.4	20.0	14.4	15.5
	1984	5.9	14.9	20.3	18.0	10.8
Netherlands	1979	15.2	30.9	54.1	29.4	23.1
	1982	24.4	35.0	48.8	31.2	32.6
	1985	42.4	61.4	72.2	56.7	52.4
Norway	1979	2.8	4.9	4.0	3.0	4.5
	1982	2.5	4.0	4.8	2.9	3.8
	1985	2.3	11.3	18.3	10.7	6.3
Spain	1979	27.8	23.6	30.3	25.0	32.5
	1982	50.2	45.6	50.0	46.9	53.8
	1984	55.0	53.5	51.8	50.9	60.3
Sweden	1979	2.0	5.2	17.1	6.8	6.7
	1982	3.1	5.9	20.7	9.2	7.5
	1985	1.2	5.9	28.5	10.9	11.9
United Kingdom	1980	7.0	21.0	40.7	22.6	12.4
	1982	21.5	37.3	47.8	37.8	23.5
	1985	28.5	44.3	55.9	45.9	30.5
United States	1979	2.4	4.7	8.6	5.0	3.4
	1982	5.4	8.9	10.4	9.2	5.7
	1985	5.1	11.0	15.3	11.7	6.8

Source: OECD Employment Outlook, Paris, 1986.

more flexible working arrangements and to encourage adaptation of working methods to suit older workers are likely to be particularly important.

A reversal of declining participation among older workers is also likely to require a reduction in the economic incentives for withdrawal from the labour force. Provided the labour market improves and that policies to encourage the employment of older workers are put in place, a strong case can be made for phasing out the types of provisions which facilitate withdrawal from the labour market before normal retirement age. An equitable sharing of the financial burden associated with population ageing would seem to require that those who are able to work remain in the labour force up to normal retirement age, thus easing the burden on the younger segments of the labour force. Support programmes would, of course, still be required for those incapable of working due to ill health or unable to find suitable employment.

There may also be potential for increasing labour force participation beyond what is now the normal retirement age, although in the absence of systematic research on the changing health status of older persons it is difficult to assess how much the working life could be extended. Such an increase in participation would almost certainly require changes in public pension systems. Possible options include an increase in the standard pensionable age with an actuarial reduction for retirement below this age, a reduction in the earnings replacement ratio of initial pension benefits and reduced indexation of benefits. However, in view of the obviously strong preference for earlier retirement, the potential impact on the average retirement age is difficult to assess. The 1983 amendments to the social security law in the United States will phase in an increase in the normal retirement age from age 65 to age 67 between 2000 and 2022. The impact of the reform on the average age of full retirement remains to be seen, although simulations indicate that the effect is likely to be relatively marginal[18].

Nevertheless, in combination with a tighter labour market and measures to encourage employment of older workers, increasing the normal retirement age would probably contribute to increasing participation rates among the elderly. The effect of changing the normal retirement age might also be increased if such a measure were to be combined with more flexible retirement policies which would enable workers to diminish their work effort gradually over time rather than passing abruptly from work to retirement. There is a growing consensus that individual preferences and social needs would be better served by a flexible rather than a fixed retirement age, and survey evidence from a number of countries indicates a relatively high propensity for part-time work among the elderly[19]. In view of the fact that postponement of retirement on any appreciable scale would have a substantial impact on the social security financing burden, the question of promoting increased labour force participation by older persons merits careful consideration. In this context, assessment of the effects of raising the normal retirement age or introducing flexible retirement should include evaluation of possible adverse consequences for vulnerable groups of older persons such as the sick and the unemployed, and possible repercussions on other social programmes, such as disability benefits.

As yet, there is little sign in most OECD countries of developments which might foster increased participation by older workers. The United States is the only country to have legislated for an increase in the normal pensionable age as the population ages more rapidly after the turn of the century. Indeed, in many European countries the trend has been towards facilitating earlier retirement and so far there is little indication of a reversal of current policy. Since the institutional changes and social consensus which would be a prerequisite for a change in retirement policies are likely to take a considerable time to achieve, and since modification of retirement norms is likely to be a relatively slow process, any reorientation of policies would need to be started well in advance of the rapid population ageing which will begin after the turn of the century.

Chapter 8

ISSUES IN HEALTH CARE POLICY

Public expenditure on health care has grown rapidly in OECD countries over the past quarter century, increasing its share of GDP from an average of 2.6 per cent in 1960 to 5.9 per cent in 1984[20]. Although the proportion of elderly people in the population rose quite substantially in many countries in this period, demographic factors were a relatively minor factor in expenditure growth. The future development of health care costs is also likely to be influenced by a range of factors other than demographic change. This chapter discusses the likely influences on public health care expenditure over the next several decades, the types of policy measures being adopted to control cost increases and the specific issues raised by prospective growth in the numbers of elderly people. Since health care policy is the subject of a number of separate OECD reports, either recent or forthcoming, what follows is only a summary of the main issues[21].

Past Growth of Public Health Care Expenditure

Analysis of the factors which have contributed to the growth of health care expenditure in the past may provide some guidance to possible future developments. Table 29 shows a disaggregation of the growth of public health care expenditure in the seven major OECD countries over the period 1960-1984. Of the 13.9 per cent annual average growth in nominal expenditure, 7.0 per cent was due to increases in health care prices and 5.6 per cent to increases in utilisation and intensity of services per person. By contrast, demographic changes, including growth of the total population and changes in age structure, accounted for only 0.8 per cent of growth. Of the 7.0 per cent increase in health care prices, 6.8 per cent was due to general economic inflation. A similar pattern of expenditure growth has been found in other OECD countries[22].

Aside from the influence of general economic inflation, therefore, the single most important factor affecting health expenditure growth has been increases in the utilisation and intensity of care. Such increases are related to a complex set of factors. The open-ended nature of health care financing systems, the autonomy of health care professionals in choosing the type and

quantity of care provided, and increasing demand due to advances in medical technology have been identified as being particularly important in this context[23]. The coverage of public health care systems expanded rapidly in the 1960s and early 1970s, but this factor has diminished in importance in recent years, as most OECD countries have achieved universal or near-universal coverage. Since utilisation/intensity is calculated as a residual it also reflects any factors which are not adequately controlled for by the relative price and demographic variables, although these are likely to be of minor importance[23].

The growth of public health care expenditure has slowed appreciably since the mid-1970s, although its share of GDP has continued to expand in many countries[23]. The budgetary constraints imposed by economic recession in this period have led to the implementation of a range of policies aimed at restraining the expansion of costs. Real per capita health benefits, reflecting utilisation and intensity of care, have grown more slowly than previously, although such growth has remained the single major cause of increasing expenditure.

Prospects for Health Care Expenditure in the Future

As shown in Part II, the projected impact of demographic factors on public health expenditure varies considerably across countries (Table 19). In most of the European countries examined, the projected increase in expenditure is modest, since the effect of population ageing is generally offset by a decline in the total population. This effect is particularly marked in Belgium, Denmark and Germany where a slight reduction in absolute expenditure is projected. By contrast, expenditure is projected to increase quite rapidly in Australia, Canada, Japan and the United States. Differences in the projected rate of expenditure growth also reflect variations in the extent to which health care spending is concentrated on the elderly, although, as noted earlier, caution should be exercised in comparing age-expenditure ratios across countries.

When projected trends in the working-age population are taken into account, as in Table 30, the impact of

Table 29. Decomposition of public health expenditure growth in seven major OECD countries, 1960-1984

Annual compound growth rates (%)

	Nominal expenditure	GDP deflator	Health prices	Relative prices	Real expenditure	of which	
						Demography	Utilisation/ intensity per person
Canada	12.5	6.1	5.6	−0.5	6.5	1.4	5.1
France	15.3	7.5	6.9	−0.6	7.9	0.8	7.0
Germany	10.1	4.3	5.6	1.2	4.2	0.4	3.8
Italy	17.6	10.5	10.5	0.0	6.5	0.5	5.9
Japan	16.8	5.7	6.0	0.3	10.2	1.1	9.1
United Kingdom	13.1	8.7	8.3	−0.4	4.4	0.3	4.1
United States	11.8	5.1	6.2	1.0	5.3	1.1	4.1
Average of above	13.9	6.8	7.0	0.1	6.4	0.8	5.6

Source: OECD, *Financing and Delivering Health Care*, Paris, 1987.

demographic change on the health care financing burden is seen to be less widely varied across countries. In Australia, Canada, Japan and the Netherlands the ratio of health care expenditure to the working-age population is projected to increase by between 51 per cent and 69 per cent over the period 1980-2040, equivalent to an annual increase of between 0.6 per cent and 0.9 per cent. This is the amount by which real earnings per worker would have to increase to cope with the pure demographic effect without any change in the average tax burden. In Denmark, Germany, Italy, Sweden and the United States the projected increases range between 31 per cent and 43 per cent, equivalent approximately to annual increases of 0.5 per cent to 0.6 per cent in the financing burden. In the remaining countries – Belgium, France, and the United Kingdom – the projected cumulative increase in the financing burden ranges from 16 per cent to 23 per cent, with annual increases of between 0.25 and 0.3 per cent.

For many of the countries examined, these growth rates represent quite a sizeable cumulative increase in the resources required to finance health care systems, purely as a result of demographic change. Any increase in utilisation and intensity of care per person, leading to an increase in real benefits per capita, and any increase in health service prices over and above the general rate of inflation would add to the financing burden. For instance, as shown in Table 30, if real health care costs per capita were to rise at the same rate as in the period 1975-84, this would lead to a dramatic increase in the financing burden in many countries. The increase is particularly marked in the case of Belgium, France and Japan, where the assumed rate of growth of real benefits is over 4.0 per cent per annum. But even in countries such as Australia, Germany and the United States, where the assumed growth in real benefits is 1.5 per cent per annum, the financing burden is approximately trebled.

Table 30. Projected change in health care financing burden 1980-2040 under alternative assumptions about growth in real per capita benefits

	Projected growth 1980-2040 (1980 = 100)		Growth in real earnings per worker required to finance additional expenditure[a]	
	Health expenditure	Population 15-64	Compound growth (1980 = 100)	Average annual compound growth (%)
	Real per capita benefits fixed at 1980 levels			
Australia	240	159	151	0.69
Belgium	99	85	116	0.25
Canada	218	129	169	0.88
Denmark	95	70	136	0.51
France	119	97	123	0.34
Germany	90	63	143	0.60
Italy	108	77	140	0.57
Japan	146	91	160	0.79
Netherlands	137	87	157	0.76
Sweden	117	89	131	0.46
United Kingdom	121	99	122	0.34
United States	178	126	141	0.58
	Real per capita benefits increasing at same rate as in 1975-84[b]			
Australia	586	159	368	2.20
Belgium	1 101	85	1 295	4.36
Canada	566	129	439	2.50
Denmark	195	70	279	1.72
France	1 986	97	2 047	5.16
Germany	220	63	349	2.11
Italy	503	77	653	3.18
Japan	1 725	91	1 896	5.03
Netherlands	185	87	213	1.27
Sweden	433	89	487	2.67
United Kingdom	262	99	265	1.63
United States	435	126	345	2.09

a) Assuming no change in average tax rate, labour force participation rate and unemployment rate.
b) Assumed annual rates of growth are as follows: Australia 1.5, Belgium 4.1, Canada 1.6, Denmark 1.2, France 4.8, Germany 1.5, Italy 2.6, Japan 4.2, Netherlands 0.5, Sweden 2.2, United Kingdom 1.3, United States 1.5
Sources: Table 19; OECD, *Measuring Health Care 1960-1983*, Paris, 1985; OECD Secretariat estimates.

In view of the pattern of expenditure growth in the past, it is likely that health care systems will be subject to a range of cost increasing pressures in addition to demographic change in the coming decades. The key factors in the development of health care expenditure, leaving aside demographic change, will be trends in real per capita benefits and in relative prices in health care systems. These factors are themselves subject to a complex set of influences, which are often difficult to identify clearly, much less control.

Further expansion of the coverage of public health care systems is unlikely to be an important source of expenditure growth as most countries have now achieved universal or near-universal coverage of the population. The United States is an exception to the general pattern since coverage is confined to the poor and the elderly, with the remainder of the population relying heavily on occupational and private provision. However, further expansion of the public health care system does not appear to be on the policy agenda.

The emphasis in most OECD countries is now on restraining health care expenditure and achieving greater efficiency in health care systems. Most countries are currently replacing or have recently replaced cost-inducing provider payment methods with systems designed to promote a more efficient use of resources[23]. Efforts are also being made to contain a range of other effects which have contributed to the growth of expenditure in the past. Limitation of the supply of physicians, hospital beds and equipment has become increasingly common. Countries are experimenting with changes in health care delivery systems with a view to enhancing efficiency. Many countries have made marginal reductions in eligibility, either by limiting coverage for more affluent groups or reducing coverage in areas regarded as being of marginal benefit, such as spa treatments and certain pharmaceuticals. Cost-sharing measures have also been extended in recent years, although in most European countries the amounts charged to consumers remain nominal. Efforts have also been made to curb the market power of health care professionals and pharmaceutical and medical equipment suppliers.

Policies to restrain expenditure appear to have met with some degree of success. Health care price inflation in excess of overall inflation in the economy has been brought under control in a number of countries, although it continues to be a problem in others. Several countries also appear to have succeeded in virtually stabilising the growth of health expenditure relative to GDP for the time being[23]. But the longer run effectiveness of many policy measures remains uncertain. Price control policies may result in increases in the quantity of services provided or in substitution of more costly services for less costly ones. It is also unclear to what extent changes in cost-sharing and delivery arrangements will affect utilisation of services over the longer run. Moreover, the impact of expenditure restraint policies on access to care and quality of care is important and policy makers will come under pressure to ensure that measures aimed at expenditure restraint do not conflict with other objectives of health care systems.

Even assuming that universal coverage has been achieved, that more cost-effective reimbursement methods have been introduced and that a range of other cost-inducing effects have been contained, countries may still face increases in the utilisation and intensity of services as a result of advances in medical technology, changes in the health status of the population and changes in family structure.

The development of new medical technology has the potential to produce large increases in health expenditures. With the rapid advance of medical research, numerous developments capable of saving and extending lives are emerging and are likely to continue to do so. New medical procedures which improve diagnostic techniques, facilitate treatment of hitherto untreatable conditions or improve and extend the available range of treatments can potentially lead to significant increases in the utilisation and intensity of care. Moreover, many new treatments are relatively expensive. While it is important to note that not all technological advances will necessarily lead to increased expenditure – some developments in the past have proved very cost effective – the net effect has tended to be cost increasing due to extensions in the range and intensity of care. The impact of technological advances is likely to be magnified by increases in the number of very elderly people, who are the heaviest users of medical care.

It is, of course, possible that the diffusion of the more expensive technologies will be rationed in some way. Already, the availability of certain treatments and procedures, such as organ transplants, is circumscribed in some countries by budgetary constraints or limits on coverage under public health care systems. However, once a new technology is in place it is difficult to limit its use and efforts to do so are likely to pose difficult ethical problems, particularly where the benefits of a procedure are limited to a relatively small group or the marginal benefits of the treatment are unclear.

A second development which may give rise to increased health care costs is increasing life expectancy. It is possible that as a greater proportion of people survive to very old ages, the incidence of disease and illness may rise, triggering a need for additional outlays on medical care. There is considerable controversy regarding likely trends in the health status of the elderly and the effect of increasing life expectancy on morbidity patterns[24]. The assumption underlying the health expenditure projections presented in Part II, that morbidity rates by age and sex will remain constant over time, is probably quite unrealistic. However, there have been too few longitudinal studies of morbidity patterns to provide a basis for projection of how trends may change in the future.

It is possible that increased longevity will be accompanied by a rise in the prevalence of chronic disease and disablement, as improved medical techniques allow those suffering from such conditions to survive longer[25]. Such a development would increase the need for medical care and other forms of care for the elderly. Some commentators contend, however, that increasing longevity will be accompanied by a reduction in the prevalence of chronic diseases, a gradual shift in disease clusters to older ages and a compression in morbidity at the upper end of the age range[26]. Such a development could lead to savings on health care since a greater proportion of the elderly population would remain healthy into advanced old age. It is also possible that the growing awareness of the links between behaviour or lifestyle and health status may contribute to a healthier elderly population in the future. In this context it is important to note, however, that while there is evidence that healthier lifestyles can help prevent some geriatric ailments, there are others for which no preventive measures have yet been found[27].

In the absence of strong evidence one way or the other, discussion of possible trends in morbidity at older ages must remain speculative. What is clear, however, is that since the numbers of very elderly persons are increasing rapidly, unless there are major advances in the treatment of chronic diseases in the coming years there will be a growing demand for geriatric care and related social services, with consequent upward pressure on health care outlays. Indeed, such pressure is already evident in a number of OECD countries. This trend may be exacerbated by changes in family structure and in the economic role of women. With declining fertility, it is to be expected that the rate of childlessness will increase among future generations of elderly persons and, to the extent that a significant amount of care is provided by family members, the resulting lacuna may have to be filled by public services. This problem may be exacerbated by the trend towards increasing labour force participation by women, who are at present the main providers of care for elderly parents and other relatives. The higher divorce rates of recent years may also imply that in the future there will be more single elderly persons who will turn to public services for care, although this will also depend on remarriage rates. A convergence in life expectancy of men and women would provide an offset to these developments since more elderly couples will remain intact and possibly able to care for one another. A further widening of the gap in life expectancy between the sexes would, of course, have the opposite effect.

It is evident that whatever the net impact on health care expenditure of increasing longevity, the pattern of health care outlays will be altered by changes in the age structure of populations. As shown in Table 31, the current structure of health care expenditure on the different age groups implies a substantial increase in the proportion spent on care for the elderly as populations grow older. The projected shift in expenditure varies across countries, reflecting differences in the concentration of spending on the elderly at present and the extent to which the age structure is projected to change.

Table 31. **Projected changes in the proportion of public health expenditure going to population aged 65 and over**[a]

	1980	2000	2020	2040
Australia	34.5	40.2	46.4	56.0
Belgium	21.8	21.8	25.0	30.4
Canada	32.4	39.4	48.9	57.1
Denmark	40.5	41.1	49.3	57.3
France	28.4	30.0	35.8	41.1
Germany	32.7	34.1	40.0	49.4
Italy	33.2	34.3	38.9	46.8
Japan	31.3	42.4	52.5	55.9
Netherlands	37.0	41.2	49.6	60.1
Sweden	51.5	54.2	59.6	63.3
United Kingdom	42.5	43.0	45.6	54.1
United States	47.0	48.8	56.9	62.9

a) Assuming constant per capita expenditure by age.
Source: OECD Secretariat estimates.

Since the incidence of chronic illness and disablement increases with age, being particularly high among the very elderly, these projected changes in the pattern of health expenditure imply that outlays in areas such as the control of infectious diseases and treatment of traumatic occurrences such as heart attacks are likely to recede in importance relative to treatment of illnesses that are lingering, but typically not life-threatening. Gradually, one-time or episodic ailments may taper off and periodic, chronic maladies may become relatively more important. Thus, the need for long-term care and associated social support services for the elderly is likely to rise considerably. This will be in addition to the increasing demand which ageing populations will place on acute care services. The cost of responding to shifts in the pattern of demand for health care should not be under-estimated. Simply imposing a quantum increase in the elderly population on health care services which are already under financial strain could have serious consequences.

In summary, a variety of factors will be influencing the pace at which health expenditures will increase, and these factors were held aside in projections of the demographic effects on health spending presented in Part II. Although it is difficult to place precise values upon the factors discussed in this chapter, it seems likely that non-demographic forces could well add to the upward push on health outlays arising from the ageing of populations. In particular, the powerful forces of research and technology are likely to create strong pressure for additional spending that could easily equal or exceed demographic pressures. Reforms in health care payment systems and other cost-containment policies could soften the impact of demographic change and technological advances on health expenditures. However, the effect of such reforms on health care prices and utilisation rates over the long run is uncertain and it is doubtful whether real per capita costs can be held stable over a long period of time. Nevertheless, while demographic pressures appear relatively unavoidable, many of the other factors influencing health care costs are susceptible to policy intervention, and developments in health care policy will have an important impact on future expenditure trends.

Policy Issues

Reform of health care systems is already on the policy agenda in most OECD countries. As noted earlier, there is widespread concern not only with the short run budgetary objective of restraining expenditure, but also with achieving greater efficiency and cost effectiveness in the provision of health care. Such efforts take on added importance because of the demographic pressures on the horizon. In the absence of institutional reform and achievement of economies, the joint effects of population ageing and increases in per capita health care costs will impose a heavy burden on society. Areas of general concern include the provision of incentives for both health care providers and consumers to reduce inappropriate use of services and treatments, elimination of waste and excess capacity in hospital services, development of more efficient health care delivery systems, provision of effective methods of planning and evaluating the use of new technology, and possibilities for improving the health status of the population through greater use of preventive medicine and encouragement of healthier life styles. Ensuring adequate access to quality care is also a central concern of health care systems and the pursuit of efficiency raises difficult policy issues with respect to the effects on equity. Such issues receive added emphasis from the rapid progress of medical technology, which confronts policy makers with ethical dilemmas concerning the appropriate application of new treatments and techniques.

Such general issues in health care policy are the subject of a separate OECD report and it is not proposed to duplicate the discussion here[20]. The following summary of policy issues is, therefore, confined to aspects of health care provision which are of particular concern in the context of ageing populations. These include the need to adjust the supply of medical care facilities in response to demographic change, the appropriate structure of care for the elderly, the delivery of long-term care, the role of informal social networks in caring for the elderly and the financing of health care systems as the demographic structure changes.

Projected changes in the age structure of populations imply substantial shifts in the demand for different types of health care which must be planned for well in advance. The growing number of elderly persons, particularly the very elderly, will increase the need for long-term care facilities. The need for medical and paramedical staff trained in geriatric medicine and care of the elderly will also increase significantly. There is already a shortage of nursing home places and geriatric hospital beds in a number of countries, leading to inappropriate utilisation of acute care facilities for

chronically ill elderly persons; adequate day-care facilities are also lacking in many countries and shortages of medical personnel trained in the care of the elderly are quite generalised[28]. The rapid growth of the very elderly population, who are the heaviest users of such services, will exacerbate existing shortages.

To the extent that increasing demand in the area of care for the elderly can be met by shifting resources from other areas of health care, this will ameliorate the pressure on health service budgets. For example, many countries face surpluses in acute hospital capacity which might be turned to other uses. There are also wide disparities between countries in average length of hospital stay for a given diagnosis, implying that if countries with relatively long lengths of stay could achieve some reduction this would free additional bed space which might be used to meet increasing demand for nursing home facilities[29]. Policies are required now to encourage the training of physicians and other types of personnel in geriatric care and to plan the provision of appropriate care facilities. Such planning should not simply be based on an extrapolation of current patterns of care but should take place in the context of a review of the full range of options for meeting the health and social support needs of the elderly.

Health care systems throughout the OECD area are characterised by an emphasis on short-term acute care and curative medicine, with a heavy reliance on treatment in institutional settings with highly sophisticated technology. While few would dispute the benefits derived from advances in such standard medical care, there is a growing recognition that inadequate attention is being paid to long-term care for the disabled and chronically ill, to preventive medicine, to the impact of environmental and behavioural factors on health status and to the provision of care in non-institutional settings. The structure of health care provision affects the entire population, but is of particular relevance for the elderly and the need to consider options for a more broadly based approach becomes more pressing as the elderly population grows.

The prevention, treatment and management of chronic physical ailments, mental disorders and limitations of activity in the elderly populations is a relatively neglected area of medicine in many countries. For example, vast sums are spent on cardiovascular disease and cancer research, but relatively little on gerontological research and services. Yet, ironically, the latter will take on added significance as the former effort succeeds. Greater emphasis needs to be placed on adequate funding of research into diseases of the elderly and possible preventive measures. Preventive care could also be improved through the establishment of systematic health screening programmes for the elderly, through programmes to encourage a healthy diet and exercise and through programmes to improve the safety of the elderly on the roads. Such measures are being developed in some European countries, including Sweden, Germany and France, but are generally a relatively neglected area of policy.

Growth in the numbers of very elderly persons also raises important issues concerning appropriate medical intervention and use of life-sustaining medical technology. Advances in medical technology have enabled the prolongation of life in the case of illnesses which would have been untreatable a few decades ago[27]. A high proportion of medical expenditure arises from treatment given to patients during the last six months of their lives. While much curative therapy is undoubtedly beneficial to patients, the marginal gain in terms of length of survival and quality of life is often difficult to judge. Physicians and health care policy makers are increasingly faced with difficult ethical questions as to how to assess the value of additional therapy, how far expensive technology and intensive treatment should be used in sustaining the lives of terminally ill or senile patients, and to what extent such treatment should be financed out of public funds. Patients and their families are also beginning to question the notion that life should be sustained as long as possible, regardless of the quality of the additional period of existence[27]. There are no easy answers to such questions and the dilemmas are likely to become increasingly acute as medical technology advances and the numbers of very elderly people increase.

The need for long-term care will expand considerably as the elderly population grows and the provision of such care constitutes one of the principal challenges for health care policy over the coming decades. The incidence of chronic illness and disability is much higher among the elderly than among younger age groups and is particularly high among the very elderly. For example, in the United States within the non-institutionalised population, limitations of activity in 1981 were twice as frequent among those aged 65 and over as among those aged 45 to 64; in 1979, those aged 85 and over were eight times more likely than those aged 65 to 74 to require assistance in performing basic daily activities such as bathing, dressing and eating[30].

The extent and nature of long-term care services vary greatly across OECD countries and it is therefore difficult to generalise about appropriate policies. The large majority of elderly people in all OECD countries live in the community, but there are wide disparities in rates of institutionalisation and in relative use rates of medically-oriented institutions and non-medical institutions[31]. In the United States most of the long-term care facilities are nursing homes, while the majority of long-term care institutions in France, Germany, the Netherlands and the United Kingdom are old age homes. Home care is used widely in Sweden and the United Kingdom, while some European countries, including France and Germany, also provide a relatively large proportion of long-term care in either acute hospitals or psychiatric hospital wards. The Netherlands, Sweden and the United Kingdom make considerable use of sheltered housing stock, while Denmark,

the Netherlands and the United Kingdom also rely heavily on use of day care centres[28].

Notwithstanding cross-national variations in the structure of long-term care, there appear to be a number of common problems. There is widespread concern over the inappropriate use of acute care facilities for long-term care. This appears to result partly from the structure of health care coverage, whereby long-term care in nursing homes or other settings is only partially covered by insurance in many countries, while hospitalisation is fully covered in most cases. Shortages of nursing home space and non-medical care facilities are also a contributing factor in some countries. A number of countries are now attempting to convert excess acute care facilities into nursing homes, and other facilities, such as hospices, old age homes and day care centres, are also being developed.

There is increasing interest in non-institutional alternatives for the provision of long-term care. All countries are attempting to increase the use of community care and home care. In some countries, such as Denmark and Sweden, home and community-based care networks are already well developed whereas in others, such as Canada and the United States, much heavier use is made of institutional care. Some European countries now use formal screening mechanisms to control admissions to long-term care facilities. Several, including Germany, Sweden and the United Kingdom are experimenting with financial assistance to relatives providing care.

The goal of maintaining the elderly in their own homes and communities is clearly a desirable one from the point of view of quality of life and social integration of the elderly, provided the necessary range of services can be made available. A constraint which currently limits the feasibility of home or community-based care is the absence of adequate services, personnel and suitable housing to meet the needs of the elderly. Such services range from medical care and physical therapy to aid with everyday chores and companionship. Suitable housing, including sheltered housing and structural modification to suit the needs of the frail and disabled is also important. Many of tomorrow's elderly will have the financial resources to pay for care outside of institutions, but will be unable to remain in the community unless the necessary array of services can be provided. It must be emphasized, however, that for patients with greater levels of disability and more extensive medical care requirements, institutional care will be necessary. A key challenge in formulating long-term care policy will be to develop a well-coordinated system of medical, paramedical, social and other support services to enable the elderly to remain self-sufficient for as long as possible, while providing more intensive care for those who need it. A widespread shortcoming in existing care structures is lack of co-ordination between the different types of service, due largely to fragmented systems of administration and funding.

One of the objectives underlying increased emphasis on home and community-based care is the achievement of savings on long-term care. Where home care substitutes for institutional care, such savings may well be realised. But it will be difficult to establish new home care programmes or extend health insurance coverage to home care while at the same time limiting use to patients coming out of hospitals or nursing homes. Others already at home, but lacking certain services, will have a legitimate claim on the new programme. Thus, the total cost of care relative to the *status quo* may rise if the overall quantity of subsidised services jumps. Of course, filling in gaps in the care structure and improving the quality of care is a desirable end in itself, but it may also be costly if the goal of horizontal equity among those in need is maintained.

Informal support systems – mainly family members – play a major role in caring for the elderly in the community. Such care is most often provided by daughters, daughters-in-law and wives. In the future the number of relatives available to provide daily care is likely to diminish because of declining family size and an increase in the proportion of women taking paid employment. However, policies towards informal care have a key role to play in the evolution of caring networks. Several European countries already have systems of paying relatives who care for the elderly. The extension of this practice to other countries would provide an incentive for family care, which may be particularly important in situations where the potential care giver has to relinquish or diminish employment in order to provide care. The availability of financial support is likely to become more important as life expectancy increases and caring for an elderly relative over a long period of time may put strain on the family's resources. Family care also needs to be backed up by social and health services such as health visitors, day care centres, day hospitals, outpatient care and respite care.

Possibilities for encouraging the development of new types of informal care networks and quasi-formal networks also need to be examined. For example, if there are fewer relatives available to provide care, the gap might be filled to some extent by encouraging the elderly to form family-type units or to engage in self-help activities[32]. It must be recognised, however, that while such networks might function well in the case of relatively autonomous elderly persons, they are unlikely to be adequate in cases where an individual requires more extensive care over a long period. Another innovative way of delivering care, which has developed in Sweden and is being tested in Norway, is the use of rural postmen to check on elderly people and arrange social services where needed[28]. Encouragement of voluntary services in the provision of long-term care and housing is also receiving increased attention in a number of countries.

The financing of long-term care is a matter of growing concern, given the potentially large expansion of demand due to growth of the very elderly population and changing family structures. Key issues in this context are the role of financing systems in providing incentives for increased use of non-institutional long-term care services, and the appropriate mix between public and private financing. Existing financing arrangements vary considerably between countries, but a relatively common feature is that care is hospitals is financed fully or very extensively by public health insurance, whereas care in nursing homes and non-institutional care receive more limited coverage. Many countries are now reviewing options for encouraging lower cost methods of providing quality care through changes in the financing system. This relates to the more general problem of changing financial incentives for physicians and hospitals to discourage over-utilisation and waste. The apportionment of financial responsibility between different levels of government also has a bearing on the structure of care. It is quite common for medical services for the elderly to be financed by state or regional authorities, whereas non-medical services such as old age homes, home helps and other social welfare measures are financed by local authorities, with some reimbursement from regional or state authorities. It is quite possible that such structures create incentives for more extensive use of medical services to care for the elderly than would be the case under less fragmented financing systems.

The issue of private sector financing of long-term care has attracted particular interest in the United States. Options being discussed include home equity conversion (reverse mortgages), private long-term care insurance, and increased public health insurance premiums for the well-off elderly. This issue has received less attention in other countries, but policy-makers everywhere will be faced with the problem of deciding how the health care costs of a growing elderly population will be financed. The basic question here runs through the entire discussion concerning the impact of a changing age structure on the financing of social programmes: how the cost should be distributed between the elderly population and the working population. Financing additional expenditure will almost certainly require increased taxation, but there is potential for requiring the elderly who can afford it to contribute to health care financing through health insurance premiums or increased cost-sharing. The alternative may be to cut benefits across the board or to increase taxes steeply. At the same time, however, it will be essential to protect the lower income elderly from undue financial strain, to ensure that those who need long-term care are not exposed to the risk of impoverishment and to ensure that inability to pay is not a barrier to access to quality care.

Chapter 9

ISSUES IN PENSION POLICY

Past Growth of Public Pension Expenditure

Public pension expenditure in OECD countries has grown very rapidly over the past two and a half decades, more than doubling its average share of GDP between 1960 and 1984, and becoming the largest single item in the public budget in most countries. While the pattern of expenditure growth has varied over time and between countries, increases in outlays are, on average, attributable in approximately equal parts to demographic factors, increases in the coverage of pension systems and increases in the average real benefits. Details of this development are taken up in a separate OECD report[18]. The major point of interest in the context of the present discussion is that increases in the elderly population, on their own, would have led to quite modest expenditure growth. Changes in programme coverage and increases in average real benefits, which to a large extent reflect policy decisions to expand public schemes, have been the dominant source of growth.

Given the extent to which pension expenditures have substantially outstripped the growth of the elderly population in the past, it is important to consider what likelihood there is that changes in system coverage and average per capita benefits will add to demographic pressures in the future, and what policy options are available for coping with the impact of population ageing. Since the development of public pension schemes is the subject of a separate OECD report, the main issues need only be summarised briefly here.

Sources of Future Expenditure Growth

In addition to increases in the elderly population, the other major factor leading to growth of pension expenditures in many countries will be maturation of the pension system. The importance of the maturation factor, its speed and its sources will vary between countries, depending on the structure of the social security system, the time which has elapsed since its introduction and the time lag since changes in coverage, eligibility or benefit regulations. While it is difficult to gauge precisely how far the public pension schemes in the various OECD countries are from maturity, it is possible to identify some important sources of increase in the average benefit level and in the proportion of elderly persons receiving benefits.

The majority of countries operate social insurance pension schemes, whereby pensions are related to some measure of previous earnings and to the contribution history of the individual. Such schemes tend to have a lengthy maturation period, during which full pension entitlements are slowly built up as successive cohorts retire having spent more of their working life in the system. Thus, there may be a time lag of three or four decades between the establishment of a new scheme and the time when maximum pensions first become payable, with a further long period intervening before all pensioners are drawing maximum benefits. The average benefit level will continue to increase in many OECD systems because the prescribed contribution period for receipt of full benefits has not yet elapsed, or because improvements made in the benefit structure in the affluent years of the 1960s and early 1970s have not yet had their full effect. Thus, many pension schemes will not begin to pay out full benefits to new retirees until the 1990s or later and it will be another 30 to 40 years before all beneficiaries are potentially in receipt of full benefits.

In addition to the effects of system maturation, average real pensions will increase over time as a result of the methods of calculating initial benefits and indexing benefits in payment. Since the initial benefit is, in most systems, calculated according to some formula based on previous earnings, average real pension levels will rise as productivity grows. Indexation of benefits already in payment to the real earnings of the working population further strengthens the link between productivity growth and benefit levels since such indexation arrangements cause benefits to rise in line with earnings. Indexation of benefits to consumer prices reduces the rate of increase in benefits relative to earnings during periods when inflation is lower than productivity growth but has the reverse effect during periods of high inflation and low productivity growth. However, even where pensions are not indexed to earnings there is likely to be strong pressure to maintain benefit levels approximately in line with the living standards of the working population.

The proportion of the elderly population receiving benefits will also rise in most pension systems as a result of the extension of coverage to new groups in recent decades and due to increases in labour force participation rates of those already covered. Over the past several decades coverage of public pension schemes has been extended to groups such as the self-employed, part-time workers, and persons outside the labour force. Female labour force participation rates have also risen considerably over time, with the result that an increasing proportion of women are gaining pension entitlements in their own right. Since the time-lag between enlarged coverage of a pension system and eligibility for benefits can stretch over an entire working life, the full impact of extensions made in recent decades will not be felt for some time to come.

The current trend towards earlier retirement in OECD countries represents another important source of increases in the proportion of beneficiaries. Although the normal pension age has, with a few exceptions, remained unchanged since the 1940s, an increasing number of countries have introduced the option of earlier or flexible retirement in various circumstances. While such provisions initially tended to be limited to workers in arduous occupations and to those with disabilities, access to earlier retirement has been extended considerably in recent years. This trend has received added impetus in the period since the mid-1970s, when early retirement measures have been viewed as a means of alleviating unemployment by encouraging older workers to withdraw from the labour force to make room for younger ones.

Early retirement claims have risen rapidly in the majority of OECD countries since the 1960s, leading to a decrease in the average retirement age[18]. This trend is also reflected in the falling labour force participation rates of older workers discussed earlier. While participation rates in the 65 and over age group are already so low as to leave little room for further reduction in many countries, additional declines in participation rates of the 55-64 age group could have a considerable impact on the number of beneficiaries.

In all, a range of factors will tend to push up average real pension levels and/or the proportion of the elderly population receiving benefits over the next several decades. As such, pension expenditures are likely to increase more rapidly than demographic change alone would imply, thus increasing the financial burden on the working population. Table 32 shows the increases in real earnings per worker necessary to finance the additional pension expenditure due to demographic change alone. In other words, this scenario assumes that average real benefits remain constant and that the employed population varies exactly in line with the population of working age. The necessary increases in real earnings per annum range from a modest 0.5 per cent in the United Kingdom and 0.6 per cent in Sweden to 1.4 per cent in Canada and 1.6 per cent in Japan. This scenario implies that the average replacement rate of pensions relative to earnings would decrease substantially over time. Alternatively, if gross average pension replacement rates were to be held constant, implying that average benefits would keep pace with average earnings, this would lead to substantial increases in contribution rates and tax rates. And if average benefits grew faster than average earnings as a result of system maturation, the projected increases in tax rates would be higher still.

Policy Issues

As discussed earlier, demographic pressures on pension systems may be moderated to some extent by exogenous factors. Pension systems financed wholly or partially on a pay-as-you-go basis, as is the case in most countries, are sensitive to labour market developments. High unemployment reduces both the number of contributors to pension schemes and national wealth. It is also likely to swell the number of beneficiaries since older workers tend to withdraw from the labour market as employment opportunities decrease and they may actually be encouraged to withdraw in order to free jobs for younger workers. In the most recent economic recession retirement benefits have also been used as an income maintenance device for unemployed older workers.

Increases in labour force participation rates would also ease the problem of financing pension schemes. Participation trends of key groups such as women, the young and the elderly are relatively sensitive to the state of the labour market and improved employment prospects could be expected to encourage increased participation. More buoyant labour markets could also lead to increased immigration of workers. However, while

Table 32. **Projected change in pension financing burden, 1980-2040**[a]

	Projected growth 1980-2040 (1980 = 100)		Growth in real earnings per worker required to finance additional expenditure[b]	
	Pension expenditure	Population 15-64	Compound growth (1980 = 100)	Average annual compound growth (%)
Australia	288	159	181	1.0
Belgium	134	85	158	0.8
Canada	304	129	236	1.4
Denmark	124	70	177	0.9
France	172	97	177	0.9
Germany	126	63	200	1.2
Italy	134	77	174	0.9
Japan	229	91	252	1.6
Netherlands	160	87	184	1.0
Sweden	123	89	138	0.6
United Kingdom	130	99	131	0.5
United States	215	126	171	0.9

a) Assuming constant real per capita benefits.
b) Alternatively, if average real benefits were to rise in line with productivity, these are the tax increases required to finance the additional expenditure due to demographic change.
Source: Table 19.

increases in participation rates raise the number of contributors to pension schemes they also ultimately swell the number of beneficiaries.

Many pension schemes are sensitive to the rates of change of nominal and real earnings. Where the indexation system and/or the benefit formula causes a lag between rates of change in earnings and rates of change in benefit levels, the replacement ratio of benefits relative to earnings decreases when the rate of change in wage levels increases and vice versa[18]. Thus, an upturn in economic performance would ease the problem of financing future pension expenditure. Conversely, poor economic performance would add to the financing burden on the active population.

Since long-term economic trends are highly uncertain, it would be unwise to rely on the possibility of favourable development to cope with pressures on pension systems. To delay reforming pension schemes in the hope that economies will prove buoyant enough to cope with projected expenditure increases would be to run the risk of putting future generations of retirees at a severe disadvantage. Reform of pension schemes requires a long lead time in order to allow future beneficiaries the necessary information to plan for retirement.

A second exogenous factor which will affect pension system financing is the degree of budgetary restructuring which takes place in response to changes in the age structure of populations. Reductions in expenditure on education and other programmes serving the young would provide a partial offset to increases in expenditure on the elderly. However, as discussed earlier, the capacity to restructure public social expenditure should not be over-estimated. Moreover, to the extent that some restructuring does take place, pension systems will be competing for resources with other programmes serving the elderly, particularly health care systems.

In view of the uncertainty surrounding possible exogenous offsets to increasing financial pressures on pension schemes, many OECD countries are turning their attention to reform of public pension systems. However, reform proposals are directed mainly to coping with current and medium-term financial problems, with less concern directed towards long-term demographic problems. Furthermore, the current tendency is to implement marginal changes in pension systems rather than completely overhaul existing structures[18].

The fundamental policy issue facing OECD countries in the light of projected increases in pension expenditures is straightforward. If the increases in tax and contribution rates necessary to cope with demographic change and system maturation are deemed too high, then future expenditure growth has to be reduced. There are only two strategies available for achieving this: benefit levels can be reduced relative to what they would otherwise have been and/or the number of beneficiaries can be reduced. The amount of the reduction in beneficiary or benefit levels is a matter of political judgement. In countries where tax and contribution burdens are still relatively low, there may be more scope for increasing tax burdens. In others, some increase in tax burdens may be acceptable if coupled with pension system reforms which place some of the burden of adjustment on the retired population.

The economic status of the elderly population relative to other age groups also has an important bearing on reform strategies. Cross-national studies indicate that the relative income position of the elderly population has improved considerably over the past two decades, largely as a result of the increased generosity of public pension schemes. Evidence for selected OECD countries shows that the elderly have incomes ranging between 75 and 90 per cent of the national average income and their vulnerability to poverty has declined appreciably over time[33]. At the same time it must be underlined that there are important income disparities within the elderly population. The very old are generally much less well-off than the recently retired, and elderly women, particularly single or widowed women, are also significantly more vulnerable to economic need than other elderly persons[33].

The economic status of the elderly may change in several ways in the future. In countries where public pension schemes are still immature, average income levels of retirees will rise as maturity is approached. Sources of private retirement income are becoming more important in most OECD countries. The expanding coverage of occupational pension schemes is particularly important in this context and it seems likely that an increasing proportion of elderly will have access to occupational pensions in the future. Private savings may increase as a result of uncertainty about trends in public pension provisions, and increasing ratios of home ownership will also raise the average wealth of the elderly in some countries. These developments will, however, affect mainly the higher income groups. Lower income groups generally have less access to occupational pension schemes and less capacity to save for old age. Thus, while the average income and wealth position of the elderly may improve further, income disparities within the elderly population may increase. This trend could be exacerbated by increases in the proportion of very elderly persons, who tend to be more vulnerable to economic insecurity. In all, current trends suggest that there is likely to be some scope for reducing the growth of pension expenditures through changes in benefit levels and/or eligibility. But at the same time it will be necessary to take steps to improve the position of the low-income elderly groups.

The adjustment of future benefit levels can be achieved by reducing the replacement rate of initial benefits and/or by reducing indexation. A number of countries have altered their indexation formulae in recent years to retard benefit adjustments, to reduce the adjustments or to weaken the link between benefits and earnings. Germany has recently changed from indexation of benefits to gross earnings to indexation to net earnings. This has the advantage of progressively reducing the growth rate of benefits as social security contribution rates rise, thus spreading the impact of demographic pressure between the working and retired populations. Both Japan and the United Kingdom have recently introduced reforms which will curb the growth of benefit replacement ratios in the future but which do not affect current pensioners.

As the merits of alternative benefit reform strategies are discussed at length in a separate OECD report, the main issues are only mentioned here[18]. While changing the indexation procedure has the advantage of producing an immediate effect on expenditure, it also carries the risk of producing economic hardship among the less well-off elderly who depend on public pension schemes for the bulk of their income. Moreover, a change from wage indexation to price indexation has, after a transition period, no effect on the growth of expenditure in systems where benefits are related to previous earnings. Although benefits in payment will remain constant in real terms, the average benefit level will rise over time in line with real earnings because of the link between initial benefits and earnings. Reducing the replacement ratio of initial benefits has the advantage of reducing the growth of expenditure over the long term. And provided the change is announced well in advance of implementation, it allows future beneficiaries to plan accordingly during their working lives.

Reductions in benefit levels provided under public schemes may need to be accompanied by policy measures to encourage the spread of occupational benefits and private saving for retirement. Occupational and private saving provisions already exist in many OECD countries and the expansion of such provisions is being quite widely discussed. It must be emphasized, however, that experience has shown the promotion of private sector arrangements to require substantial tax concessions, which will offset some of the saving on reduced public sector provisions. Private arrangements are also likely to demand extensive public regulation if large negative impacts on income distribution and economic performance are to be avoided.

Reductions in benefits provided by earnings-related schemes may also need to be accompanied by the introduction or extension of basic income support provisions. Such provisions could help to improve the income position of vulnerable groups such as the very elderly and lone elderly women, as well as offsetting the adverse distributional impacts of private retirement provisions.

The main strategy for reducing the number of beneficiaries is to increase the retirement age. This would reduce or eliminate the necessity to cut benefit levels. The only country to adopt such a strategy to date has been the United States, but retirement age policy is under discussion in other countries. In Europe the poor labour market situation in recent years has led to a tendency to encourage elderly workers to leave the labour market rather than to stay longer. Obviously an increase in retirement age would not be an attractive solution to problems of pension systems unless the labour market improved. However, shrinkage or slower growth of the working population towards the end of the century may lead to tighter labour market conditions and increase the feasibility of raising the retirement age. As with benefit changes, however, changes in retirement age should be announced well in advance in order to enable individuals to plan accordingly.

An increase in the standard retirement age might also be accompanied by greater flexibility in retirement arrangements, enabling individuals to gradually move from full-time work to full retirement. A major problem with devising flexible retirement arrangements is achieving an equitable and efficient balance between the provision of adequate benefits and incentives to continue working[18]. Whereas a high benefit level between, say, ages 60 and 65 would reduce work incentives, a lower benefit level could encourage postponement of full retirement but might cause hardship for those who have to withdraw earlier from the labour market due to disability, long-term unemployment or lack of suitable skills. The challenge will be to provide suitable incentives to work for the elderly who are capable of continued employment, while ensuring that vulnerable groups are protected from undue hardship.

Changes in the method of financing pension systems are under discussion in many countries. Although the financing mode does not affect the level of pension expenditures, it may influence the amount of resources available to pay for increased outlays. At present, pension schemes in OECD countries are financed largely on a pay-as-you-go basis. Thus, the current working population finances the pensions of the retired population, on the understanding that their pensions will in turn be paid for by future generations of workers. Concern with this method of financing arises from two main sources. Firstly, pay-as-you-go systems are vulnerable to demographic shifts. When, as will happen in most OECD countries in the coming decades, the numbers of elderly increase rapidly while the numbers of working age people are falling or remaining constant, the financial burden on the working population increases. Secondly, high and rising social security contribution rates have raised concerns over possible distortion of factor prices with adverse effects on the demand for labour.

The possibility of changing from pay-as-you-go financing to funding or partial funding of pension systems has recently received attention in some countries. However, as noted in an OECD report, a major obstacle to such a change would appear to be the double burden imposed on the transitional generation, which would have to pay for its own retirement through the funded system and for the current generation of retirees under the pay-as-you-go system[34]. Any positive effect on capital formation and real income would be enjoyed by the next generation, raising issues of intergenerational equity. An additional concern arises from the fact that because the accumulated fund would have to be very large to produce an income sufficient to finance future pension commitments, there could be adverse effects on the supply of capital for the private sector, on interest rates, and on the management of the money supply[35]. Empirical research has produced ambiguous results concerning the economic effects of a change to funding, and so far the proposal has received very limited support.

Many countries have enlarged the pension contribution base in recent years through measures such as raising or abolishing contribution ceilings and extension of the contribution base to remunerations previously not subject to contribution. The possibility of enlarging the contribution base to include items such as profits, interest revenues and depreciation is being considered in some countries, and the options of taxing social security benefits and eliminating special tax exemptions for the elderly are also under discussion. The feasibility of moving from a system of earmarked social security contributions to funding from general tax revenues or value added tax is under review in several countries. To date, however, no country has undertaken a major reform of the financing system.

NOTES AND REFERENCES

1. OECD, Educational data bank.

2. OECD, *Social Expenditure 1960-1990*, Paris, 1985.

3. Ermisch, John. F., *The Political Economy of Demographic Change*, London, Heinemann, 1983, Chapter 4.

4. Ermisch, *ibid.*

5. See, for instance, Habib, Jack, "The Economy and the Aged" in Robert H. Binstock and Ethel Shanas (eds.), *Handbook of Aging and the Social Sciences* (second edition), New York, Van Nostrand Reinhold Company, 1985, pp. 479-502; Clark, Robert L. and Joseph J. Spengler, *The Economics of Individual and Population Aging*, Cambridge, Cambridge University press, 1980, Chapter 9.

6. See, for instance, Clark and Spengler, *op.cit.*, Chapter 9; Habib, *op.cit.*; Ashenfelter, O., "The Economic Impact of an Older Population: A brief survey" in A.J.J. Gilmore *et al.* (eds.) *Ageing: A Challenge to Science and Society*, Oxford: Oxford University Press, 1982, pp. 333-40.

7. Habib, *op.cit.*

8. See Habib, *op.cit.*; OECD, *Socio-Economic Policies for the Elderly*, Paris, 1979.

9. See, for instance, Clark and Spengler, *op.cit.*, Chapter 9; Palmer, John L. and Gould, Stephanie G. "The Economic Consequences of an Aging Society", *Daedalus*, 115:1, 1986, pp. 295-323.

10. See Habib, *op.cit.*; Russell, Louise B., "The Macroeconomic Effects of Change in the Age Structure of the Population": in Maurice B. Ballabon (ed.), *Economic Perspectives: An Annual Survey of Economics*, Amsterdam: OPA, 1979, Vol. 3.

11. OECD, *Employment Outlook*, Paris, 1983, p. 19.

12. See Rix, Sara E. and Paul Fisher, *Retirement-Age Policy. An International Perspective*, New York, Pergamon Press, 1982, p. 55.

13. See Ermisch, *op.cit.*

14. OECD, *Employment Outlook*, 1985, p. 37.

15. See OECD, *Labour Force Statistics*, Paris, 1986.

16. Rones, Philip L., "The Labour Market Problems of Older Workers", *Monthly Labor Review*, 106:5, 1983, pp. 3-12.

17. See *Wall Street Journal*, 10 September 1986.

18. OECD, *Reforming Public Pensions*, Paris, 1988.

19. See, for instance, Morrison, Malcolm H., "The Aging of the U.S. Population: Human Resource Implications", *Monthly Labor Review*, 106:5, 1983, pp. 13-19; Ogawa, Nachiro and Suits, David B., "Retirement Policy and Japanese Workers: Some Results of an Opinion Survey", *International Labour Review*, 122:5, 1983.

20. OECD, *Financing and Delivering Health Care*, Paris, 1987.

21. *Ibid*; OECD, *Measuring Health Care 1960-1983*, Paris, 1985; Schieber, George J., "The Financing and Delivery of Health Care in OECD Countries: Past, Present and Future", paper presented at meeting on the subject "Health and Pensions Policy in the Context of Demographic Evolution and Economic Constraints", organised jointly by the Japanese Government and the OECD, Tokyo, 25 to 28 November 1985.

22. OECD, *Financing and Delivering Health Care*, *op.cit.*; OECD, *Social Expenditure 1960-1990*, *op.cit.*; Poullier, Jean-Pierre, "From Risk Aversion to Risk Rating: Trends in OECD Health Care Systems", *International Journal of Health Planning and Management*, 1987.

23. OECD, *Financing and Delivering Health Care*, *op.cit.*

24. See, for instance, Rice, Dorothy P. and Estes, Carroll L., "Health of the Elderly: Policy Issues and Challenges", *Health Affairs*, 3:4 (1984) pp. 25-49; Manton, K.C., "Changing Concepts of Morbidity and Mortality in the Elderly Population", *Millbank Memorial Fund Quarterly/Health and Society*, 60:2 (1982) pp. 183-244; Fries, J.F., "Aging, Natural Death and the Compression of Morbidity", *New England Journal of Medicine*, 303:3 (1980) pp. 130-35; Fries, J.F. and Crapo, L.M., *Vitality and Aging: Implications of the Rectangular Curve*, San Francisco: W.H. Freeman, 1981.

25. See Avorn, Jerome L. "Medicine, Health and the Geriatric Transformation", *Daedalus*, Vol. 115, No. 1, 1986, pp. 211-226; Rice and Estes, *op.cit.*

26. Fries, *op.cit.*; Manton, *op.cit.*

27. Avorn, *op.cit.*

28. United States Senate, Special Committee on Aging, *Long-Term Care in Western Europe and Canada: Implications for the United States,* Washington, U.S. Government Printing Office, 1984.

29. Poullier, Jean-Pierre, "From Kaiserliche Botschaft's Rede to Kremsmünster: Has Montesquieu's Paradox Evolved?", *Annuaire 1987*, Institut Européen de Sécurité Sociale, Leuven: Acco, 1988.

30. Rice and Estes, *op.cit.*

31. International Social Security Association, *Long-Term Care for the Elderly Provided Within the Framework of Health Care Systems*, Report presented at XXIInd General Assembly, Montreal, 2-12 September 1986.

32. See, for instance, Sussman, Marvin B., "The family life of old people" in Binstock and Shanas, *op.cit.* pp. 415-449.

33. Boyle Torrey, Barbara *et al.*, *A Comparative Study of the Economics of the Aged*, paper presented at Chair Quetelet 86 Conference on the subject of "Populations Agées et Révolution Grise", Université Catholique de Louvain, Louvain-la-Neuve, 6-10 October 1986.

34. Holzmann, Robert, "Issues in the Development of Public Pension Schemes: International and Historical Perspectives", paper presented at the meeting on the subject of "Health and Pensions Policies in the Context of Demographic Evolution and Economic Constraints", organised jointly by the Japanese Government and the OECD, Tokyo, 25 to 28 November 1985.

35. Rix and Fisher, *op.cit.*, Chapter 6.

SUMMARY OF PART III

Virtually all OECD countries will face the problem of population ageing from the early part of the next century; in a few cases demographic pressures will begin to mount much sooner. Countries will face growing fiscal burdens as expenditures increase and the working-age population shrinks or remains constant in size. However, while the evolution of programme costs and financing burdens will be determined partially by factors outside the control of policy-makers, there are areas where policy intervention could ease the problem of coping with population ageing.

Declining numbers of young dependants will to some extent offset increasing outlays for the support and care of the elderly. The greatest potential cost offset is in the area of education, where in many countries demographic change will provide scope for savings. But savings will undoubtedly be limited by structural characteristics of education systems, such as tenure rules and relative salary scales. There will also be problems of timing, because in many cases the greatest potential for saving on education seems likely to occur before pressures on pension and health care systems begin to mount. Nevertheless, in view of the fact that realisation of savings on education, and to a lesser extent on other programmes catering to the young, could appreciably reduce the overall growth of social expenditure, policy makers will have a strong incentive to attempt the restructuring of expenditure. In so doing, it will be necessary to balance budgetary considerations against likely resistance to reducing the scale of programmes serving the young, and against demands for services to meet new needs or to cater to needs which at present are inadequately met. Attempts at restructuring are also likely to generate tensions between central and local authorities in countries where education expenditures are under local control.

A growing economy and growing employment would obviously ease the problem of financing additional social outlays. It seems unlikely that the projected ageing of the labour force will have a significant effect on labour productivity. Secular increases in productivity would appear to be dominated by other influences, such as education, technological change and the amount of capital available per worker. However, rapid technological change would tend to reduce the productivity-enhancing effects of accumulated skill and experience on the part of older workers, and reduced mobility due to ageing of the workforce could also have an effect on productivity. Policies to retrain older workers, to update their skills, to encourage adaptation of working methods to suit older workers and to improve labour mobility could have an important impact on productivity as the workforce ages.

A key factor affecting the capacity to support a growing elderly population will be the extent to which shrinkage of the working-age population is offset by increases in the labour supply. Provided the demand for labour recovers, many countries could face labour shortages by the turn of the century. Such shortages would be exacerbated by a continuation of the trend towards declining labour force participation by older workers. Labour shortages could be satisfied in a variety of ways, including immigration, increasing participation by women and youth, and increasing participation by older workers. In the event that labour shortages materialise, the labour market is likely to be self-adjusting to a large extent. However, there is no guarantee that employers will choose the solution of encouraging increased participation by older workers. Such an increase is desirable because it would not only increase the capacity to finance social programmes, but would at the same time reduce the numbers dependant on these programmes.

It seems possible that future developments will to some extent act to reverse the decline in participation rates of older workers. The generosity of public (and probably also private) pension schemes is unlikely to increase very much over the next few decades and there may be reductions in benefit levels in some countries. Opportunities for part-time employment are also likely to continue expanding, and this may encourage a greater proportion of older people to remain in the labour market. It is probable, however, that such factors would need to be reinforced by policy changes such as provision of retraining, increases in the official retirement age, less than full indexation of pensions to earnings, or reductions in the earnings-replacement rate of initial pension benefits. There is also a strong case to be made for removing incentives to early retirement.

The main problems with policies which seek to persuade workers to remain active for longer are likely to be those of, first, ensuring sufficient flexibility in working conditions and pension provisions to enable the transition from work to retirement to take place smoothly; and second, of distinguishing in an equitable way between those workers who might wish, or be willing to increase their participation and those who, for reasons of health or inability to find appropriate work, are unable to do so. The first group requires incentives, the latter needs support. In particular the institutional changes and social consensus which would be pre-requisites for such policies may take some time to achieve, and a beginning needs to be made well in advance of the demographic bulge which will occur after the turn of the century.

There are also limitations to how far the process of extending the worklife can go. Lengthening life expectancy may provide some potential for postponing retirement beyond the current standard retirement age – 65 in most countries – but this will depend on whether disability rates decrease as mortality rates fall. It would also be unrealistic to call for a lengthening of the working life without efforts to redesign jobs to fit the needs and capabilities of older workers. For instance, ways of utilising the skills and experience of older workers either on a part-time basis or in a different job in the same firm could be explored. In short, it will be necessary to review the array of labour market and retirement policies to find ways to encourage participation of older workers. An important issue facing policy makers in this context is whether such measures should simply seek to facilitate participation by those who wish to work, or whether there may also be justification for recourse to involuntary measures, such as reducing benefit levels.

Reform of health care and pension systems is already on the policy agenda in most OECD countries as a result of current budgetary problems and because of a perceived need to improve the efficiency and effectiveness of programmes. Projected demographic pressures add to the necessity for reforms which will reduce the future growth of costs and effectively meet the needs of a growing elderly population. To the extent that reforms are not undertaken, demographic pressures are likely to be reinforced by other cost-inducing effects. Demographic change will increase the burden of both pensions and health care costs on the working population. But it may also be necessary for the elderly population to assume a share of the increased burden. The central questions are how much sharing there should be, and how this should be achieved. Success in restructuring social expenditure and in increasing the size of the employed population would reduce, although probably not eliminate, the need for adjustments in pension and health care systems.

Options for redistributing the financing burden between the working and retired populations include reductions in the level and/or scale of benefits and extension of the financing base to include the income of the better-off sections of the elderly population. Improvements in the relative income and wealth position of the elderly have increased the viability of such measures, although the problems of low income groups within the elderly population need to be addressed. A crucial policy issue in this context is whether the cost of adjustment to demographic pressures should be spread across the elderly population as a whole, via reductions in benefits, or whether it should be concentrated on the better-off sections of the elderly, through selective reductions in eligibility and extensions of the tax base. Changes in the method of financing pension systems – from pay-as-you-go to funding – cannot be assumed to offer any help in meeting additional costs arising from population ageing.

In the case of health care, the effects of demographic change, reinforced by advances in medical technology, can be attenuated by reforms in the financing and delivery of care. Crucial areas for reform are provider payment systems which encourage unnecessary or wasteful use of resources, and approaches to meeting the needs of the elderly and very elderly populations. The bias towards high-cost institutional care should be removed to the extent possible, and policies devised for meeting the needs of the elderly in a community setting. In this context, it should be emphasized that such needs are multi-dimensional, involving not only standard medical care but also social services, housing, and integration in the community.

Private sector arrangements are likely to emerge as an important supplement to public pension and health care programmes in some countries, and in several cases efforts are already being made to encourage the development of private sector provisions. While such arrangements can supplement public programmes and relieve some of the strain on public commitments, they cannot substitute for public provisions. Moreover, private sector initiatives are likely to require financial incentives from the public sector and to need substantial regulation in order to avoid adverse distributional consequences. Finally, increased recourse to private sector arrangements will not eliminate the need for society to transfer an increased proportion of the available resources to the elderly as populations age, although it should provide additional flexibility in deciding how additional resource requirements are to be satisfied.

Annex A

DEMOGRAPHIC PROJECTIONS

Table A.1. **Age structure of OECD populations**[a]

Millions

		1950	1980	1990	2000	2010	2020	2030	2040	2050
Australia	0-14	2.18	3.71	3.73	4.01	4.05	4.20	4.48	4.69	4.98
	15-64	5.34	9.57	11.20	12.49	13.71	14.30	14.72	15.18	15.91
	65 +	0.66	1.41	1.86	2.18	2.56	3.37	4.28	4.88	5.04
	Total	8.18	14.70	16.79	18.68	20.32	21.87	23.48	24.75	25.93
Austria	0-14	1.58	1.54	1.36	1.42	1.29	1.27	1.27	1.24	1.26
	15-64	4.63	4.80	5.06	5.02	4.97	4.82	4.45	4.22	4.16
	65 +	0.72	1.16	1.10	1.13	1.32	1.47	1.69	1.72	1.50
	Total	6.94	7.51	7.52	7.58	7.57	7.56	7.41	7.18	6.92
Belgium	0-14	1.81	1.97	1.85	1.79	1.60	1.56	1.57	1.56	1.57
	15-64	5.88	6.46	6.60	6.54	6.55	6.32	5.84	5.49	5.30
	65 +	0.95	1.42	1.39	1.44	1.54	1.70	1.94	1.97	1.80
	Total	8.64	9.85	9.84	9.76	9.69	9.58	9.35	9.02	8.67
Canada	0-14	4.09	5.53	5.52	5.65	5.31	5.58	6.01	6.38	6.88
	15-64	8.61	16.23	18.04	19.57	21.06	21.11	20.56	20.90	21.58
	65 +	1.06	2.29	3.02	3.72	4.51	6.10	7.66	7.91	7.72
	Total	13.75	24.04	26.58	28.93	30.88	32.78	34.23	35.18	36.18
Denmark	0-14	1.12	1.07	0.85	0.78	0.69	0.62	0.65	0.65	0.65
	15-64	2.76	3.32	3.43	3.41	3.23	2.93	2.60	2.31	2.18
	65 +	0.39	0.74	0.77	0.73	0.79	0.89	0.95	0.97	0.86
	Total	4.27	5.12	5.05	4.92	4.71	4.45	4.19	3.94	3.69
Finland	0-14	1.20	0.97	0.95	0.87	0.78	0.76	0.76	0.76	0.76
	15-64	2.54	3.24	3.35	3.38	3.33	3.02	2.77	2.63	2.51
	65 +	0.27	0.57	0.65	0.72	0.83	1.05	1.10	1.02	0.96
	Total	4.01	4.78	4.94	4.96	4.94	4.83	4.64	4.42	4.23
France	0-14	9.50	11.97	11.34	10.95	10.08	9.82	9.99	10.01	9.96
	15-64	27.58	34.25	36.72	37.35	38.34	36.74	34.86	33.22	32.49
	65 +	4.76	7.50	7.69	8.71	9.40	11.24	12.47	12.74	12.20
	Total	41.84	53.71	55.75	57.01	57.82	57.80	57.31	56.07	54.66
Germany	0-14	11.77	11.19	9.18	9.22	7.45	7.08	7.25	6.88	6.97
	15-64	33.54	40.83	42.32	40.19	37.51	34.14	28.86	25.92	24.62
	65 +	4.67	9.55	9.45	10.21	11.48	11.45	12.57	12.50	10.24
	Total	49.98	61.57	60.95	59.62	56.44	52.67	48.69	45.30	41.84
Greece	0-14	2.17	2.20	2.00	1.89	1.83	1.75	1.70	1.66	1.62
	15-64	4.89	6.18	6.65	6.61	6.63	6.54	6.28	5.95	5.72
	65 +	0.51	1.27	1.21	1.50	1.70	1.79	1.93	2.02	1.96
	Total	7.57	9.64	9.85	10.00	10.16	10.08	9.91	9.64	9.30
Iceland	0-14	0.04	0.06	0.06	0.06	0.05	0.05	0.05	0.06	0.06
	15-64	0.09	0.14	0.16	0.18	0.02	0.02	0.19	0.18	0.17
	65 +	0.01	0.02	0.03	0.03	0.03	0.04	0.05	0.06	0.06
	Total	0.14	0.23	0.25	0.27	0.28	0.29	0.29	0.29	0.29
Ireland	0-14	0.85	1.04	1.02	0.91	0.87	0.85	0.89	0.92	0.88
	15-64	1.80	2.00	2.28	2.58	2.79	2.85	2.83	2.77	2.71
	65 +	0.32	0.37	0.42	0.44	0.46	0.53	0.64	0.75	0.83
	Total	2.97	3.40	3.72	3.93	4.11	4.23	4.36	4.44	4.42
Italy	0-14	12.47	12.55	10.16	9.65	8.56	7.77	8.16	8.21	8.07
	15-64	30.86	36.84	39.08	38.25	37.31	35.16	31.68	28.46	27.20
	65 +	3.78	7.68	7.86	8.66	9.58	10.32	11.18	11.67	10.30
	Total	47.11	57.07	57.10	56.56	55.44	53.25	51.02	48.34	45.57
Japan	0-14	29.57	27.53	22.42	22.31	23.64	21.19	21.15	20.83	20.28
	15-64	49.73	78.88	86.36	85.68	81.24	78.40	76.55	71.86	70.59
	65 +	4.36	10.65	14.01	19.36	23.99	26.35	24.38	27.16	26.09
	Total	83.66	117.06	122.79	127.35	128.87	125.95	122.08	119.85	116.96
Luxembourg	0-14	0.06	0.07	0.07	0.07	0.06	0.06	0.07	0.06	0.07
	15-64	0.21	0.25	0.26	0.25	0.25	0.24	0.23	0.23	0.22
	65 +	0.03	0.05	0.06	0.06	0.07	0.08	0.09	0.08	0.07
	Total	0.30	0.36	0.38	0.38	0.39	0.38	0.38	0.37	0.37
Netherlands	0-14	2.96	3.16	2.68	2.76	2.48	2.34	2.38	2.25	2.27
	15-64	6.37	9.36	10.24	10.38	10.36	9.71	8.83	8.17	7.93
	65 +	0.78	1.63	1.88	2.05	2.29	2.81	3.34	3.43	2.98
	Total	10.11	14.15	14.80	15.19	15.13	14.86	14.54	13.85	13.17

		1950	1980	1990	2000	2010	2020	2030	2040	2050
New Zealand	0-14	0.56	0.85	0.77	0.79	0.76	0.73	0.72	0.70	0.70
	15-64	1.19	2.00	2.31	2.52	2.68	2.71	2.61	2.50	2.46
	65 +	0.17	0.31	0.37	0.41	0.47	0.62	0.80	0.90	0.86
	Total	1.92	3.16	3.46	3.72	3.91	4.06	4.13	4.10	4.01
Norway	0-14	0.80	0.91	0.78	0.79	0.74	0.71	0.74	0.74	0.75
	15-64	2.15	2.58	2.73	2.83	2.89	2.79	2.66	2.53	2.51
	65 +	0.31	0.60	0.68	0.65	0.65	0.78	0.89	0.97	0.91
	Total	3.27	4.09	4.19	4.27	4.28	4.29	4.28	4.24	4.17
Portugal	0-14	2.49	2.52	2.27	2.22	2.06	1.91	1.86	1.77	1.66
	15-64	5.36	5.93	6.65	6.76	6.92	6.87	6.49	6.07	5.79
	65 +	0.59	0.96	1.19	1.41	1.48	1.63	1.86	2.01	1.93
	Total	8.44	9.41	10.11	10.39	10.46	10.41	10.21	9.85	9.38
Spain	0-14	7.55	9.68	8.60	8.13	6.98	6.56	7.13	7.31	7.09
	15-64	18.29	23.65	26.01	27.01	28.11	27.78	26.09	24.16	23.34
	65 +	2.03	4.06	5.05	5.89	6.45	7.04	8.12	9.23	9.02
	Total	27.87	37.39	39.66	41.03	41.54	41.38	41.33	40.70	39.44
Sweden	0-14	1.65	1.63	1.43	1.44	1.39	1.34	1.38	1.38	1.40
	15-64	4.65	5.33	5.42	5.48	5.38	5.16	4.96	4.75	4.71
	65 +	0.72	1.35	1.48	1.38	1.43	1.71	1.76	1.78	1.66
	Total	7.02	8.31	8.33	8.30	8.20	8.20	8.09	7.91	7.77
Switzerland	0-14	1.11	1.25	1.09	1.08	0.97	0.92	0.90	0.86	0.86
	15-64	3.14	4.20	4.45	4.38	4.21	3.88	3.49	3.22	3.07
	65 +	0.45	0.88	0.96	1.10	1.33	1.55	1.65	1.60	1.40
	Total	4.69	6.33	6.50	6.55	6.51	6.34	6.05	5.68	5.34
Turkey	0-14	8.00	17.43	20.69	22.14	21.60	22.19	26.02	28.05	25.51
	15-64	12.11	25.02	34.89	43.35	52.95	59.97	64.16	68.87	74.22
	65 +	0.70	2.11	2.29	3.47	4.36	6.16	8.83	10.98	12.98
	Total	20.81	44.57	57.86	68.97	78.91	88.32	99.01	107.90	112.71
United Kingdom	0-14	11.25	11.83	10.76	11.73	11.46	11.62	11.12	10.30	10.69
	15-64	33.71	35.85	37.17	37.15	37.72	37.22	36.20	35.58	35.40
	65 +	5.40	8.33	8.54	8.28	8.41	9.49	11.27	11.78	10.63
	Total	50.37	56.01	56.47	57.15	57.59	58.34	58.60	57.66	56.72
United States	0-14	41.00	51.29	54.21	55.96	53.92	56.25	57.16	58.38	60.27
	15-64	98.88	150.74	163.94	177.21	190.15	189.84	186.15	189.76	193.47
	65 +	12.40	25.71	30.39	32.23	35.81	47.42	58.92	61.27	60.73
	Total	152.27	127.74	248.54	265.40	279.88	293.51	302.23	309.41	314.47

a) 1950 to 1980 actual numbers; 1990 to 2050 projected numbers.
Source: OECD Demographic Data File, medium fertility variant projections.

Table A.2. **Age structure of OECD populations**[a]

Per cent

		1950	1980	1990	2000	2010	2020	2030	2040	2050
Australia	0-14	26.6	25.3	22.2	21.4	19.9	19.2	19.1	19.0	19.2
	15-64	65.2	65.1	66.7	66.9	67.5	65.4	62.7	61.3	61.4
	65 +	8.1	9.6	11.1	11.7	12.6	15.4	18.2	19.7	19.4
Austria	0-14	22.7	20.5	18.1	18.8	17.0	16.8	17.2	17.3	18.2
	15-64	66.8	64.0	67.3	66.3	65.6	63.8	60.0	58.7	60.1
	65 +	10.4	15.5	14.6	14.9	17.5	19.4	22.8	23.9	21.7
Belgium	0-14	20.9	20.0	18.8	18.3	16.6	16.3	16.8	17.3	18.1
	15-64	68.0	65.6	67.0	67.0	67.5	66.0	62.4	60.8	61.1
	65 +	11.0	14.4	14.2	14.7	15.9	17.7	20.8	21.9	20.8
Canada	0-14	29.7	23.0	20.8	19.5	17.2	17.0	17.5	18.1	19.0
	15-64	62.6	67.5	67.9	67.6	68.2	64.4	60.1	59.4	59.6
	65 +	7.6	9.5	11.4	12.8	14.6	18.6	22.4	22.5	21.3
Denmark	0-14	26.3	20.8	16.8	15.8	14.7	14.0	15.5	16.6	17.6
	15-64	64.5	64.7	67.9	69.3	68.6	65.9	61.9	58.7	59.2
	65 +	9.1	14.4	15.3	14.9	16.7	20.1	22.6	24.7	23.2
Finland	0-14	29.9	20.3	19.2	17.4	15.8	15.7	16.4	17.2	17.9
	15-64	63.4	67.7	67.7	68.1	67.4	62.5	59.8	59.6	59.4
	65 +	6.6	12.0	13.1	14.1	16.8	21.7	23.8	23.1	22.7
France	0-14	22.7	22.3	20.3	19.2	17.4	17.0	17.4	17.9	18.2
	15-64	65.9	63.8	65.9	65.5	66.3	63.6	60.8	59.4	59.5
	65 +	11.3	14.0	13.8	15.3	16.3	19.5	21.8	22.7	22.3
Germany	0-14	23.5	18.2	15.1	15.5	13.2	13.4	14.9	15.2	16.7
	15-64	67.1	66.3	69.4	67.4	66.5	64.8	59.3	57.2	58.9
	65 +	9.3	15.5	15.5	17.1	20.3	21.7	25.8	27.6	24.5
Greece	0-14	28.6	22.8	20.3	18.9	18.0	17.3	17.2	17.2	17.4
	15-64	64.6	64.0	67.4	66.1	65.2	64.9	63.3	61.8	61.5
	65 +	6.7	13.1	12.3	15.0	16.8	17.8	19.5	21.0	21.1
Iceland	0-14	30.5	27.5	25.1	21.7	18.8	17.7	18.4	19.0	18.9
	15-64	61.8	62.6	64.6	67.5	70.0	68.1	63.5	60.9	60.0
	65 +	7.6	9.9	10.3	10.9	11.2	14.2	18.1	20.1	21.1
Ireland	0-14	28.6	30.4	27.5	23.2	21.0	20.1	20.4	20.7	19.9
	15-64	60.7	58.8	61.2	65.6	67.9	67.3	64.9	62.4	61.3
	65 +	10.6	10.7	11.3	11.1	11.1	12.6	14.7	16.9	18.9
Italy	0-14	26.4	22.0	17.8	17.1	15.4	14.6	16.0	17.0	17.7
	15-64	65.5	64.6	68.4	67.6	67.3	66.0	62.1	58.9	59.7
	65 +	8.0	13.4	13.8	15.3	17.3	19.4	21.9	24.2	22.6
Japan	0-14	35.3	23.5	18.3	17.5	18.3	16.8	17.3	17.4	17.3
	15-64	59.5	67.4	70.3	67.3	63.0	62.3	62.7	60.0	60.4
	65 +	5.2	9.1	11.4	15.2	18.6	20.9	20.0	22.7	22.3
Luxembourg	0-14	19.9	18.8	17.5	17.7	16.1	16.6	17.2	17.5	18.6
	15-64	70.3	67.7	67.9	65.6	65.8	63.2	60.4	60.5	61.1
	65 +	9.8	13.5	14.6	16.7	18.1	20.1	22.4	22.0	20.3
Netherlands	0-14	29.3	22.3	18.1	18.2	16.4	15.8	16.3	16.3	17.2
	15-64	62.9	66.2	69.2	68.3	68.5	65.3	60.7	59.0	60.2
	65 +	7.7	11.5	12.7	13.5	15.1	18.9	23.0	24.8	22.6
New Zealand	0-14	29.1	27.0	22.2	21.2	19.3	18.0	17.5	17.1	17.5
	15-64	61.9	63.3	66.9	67.7	68.6	66.7	63.2	61.1	61.2
	65 +	8.9	9.7	10.8	11.1	12.0	15.3	19.4	21.9	21.3
Norway	0-14	24.4	22.2	18.7	18.5	17.3	16.6	17.2	17.5	18.0
	15-64	65.9	63.1	65.1	66.3	67.6	65.2	62.1	59.7	60.1
	65 +	9.5	14.8	16.2	15.2	15.1	18.2	20.7	22.8	21.9
Portugal	0-14	29.5	26.8	22.5	21.4	19.7	18.3	18.2	18.0	17.7
	15-64	63.5	63.1	65.7	65.1	66.2	66.1	63.6	61.6	61.7
	65 +	6.9	10.2	11.8	13.5	14.1	15.6	18.2	20.4	20.6
Spain	0-14	27.0	25.9	21.7	19.8	16.8	15.9	17.2	18.0	18.0
	15-64	65.6	63.3	65.6	65.8	67.7	67.1	63.1	59.4	59.2
	65 +	7.3	10.9	12.7	14.4	15.5	17.0	19.6	22.7	22.9
Sweden	0-14	23.4	19.6	17.2	17.4	16.9	16.3	17.0	17.4	18.0
	15-64	66.3	64.1	65.0	66.0	65.6	62.9	61.3	60.1	60.6
	65 +	10.2	16.3	17.7	16.6	17.5	20.8	21.7	22.5	21.4

		1950	1980	1990	2000	2010	2020	2030	2040	2050
Switzerland	0-14	23.5	19.7	16.7	16.4	14.8	14.5	14.9	15.1	16.2
	15-64	66.8	66.5	68.5	66.9	64.7	61.1	57.8	56.7	57.6
	65 +	9.6	13.8	14.8	16.7	20.5	24.4	27.3	28.3	26.3
Turkey	0-14	38.4	39.1	35.8	32.1	27.4	25.1	26.3	26.0	22.6
	15-64	58.2	56.1	60.3	62.9	67.1	67.9	64.8	63.8	65.9
	65 +	3.3	4.7	4.0	5.0	5.5	7.0	8.9	10.2	11.5
United Kingdom	0-14	22.3	21.1	19.1	20.5	19.9	19.9	19.0	17.9	18.8
	15-64	66.9	64.0	65.8	65.0	65.5	63.8	61.8	61.7	62.4
	65 +	10.7	14.9	15.1	14.5	14.6	16.3	19.2	20.4	18.7
United States	0-14	26.9	22.5	21.8	21.1	19.3	19.2	18.9	18.9	19.2
	15-64	64.9	66.2	66.0	66.8	67.9	64.7	61.6	61.3	61.5
	65 +	8.1	11.3	12.2	12.1	12.8	16.2	19.5	19.8	19.3

a) See Table A.1.
Source: See Table A.1.

Table A.3.   **Trends in the age structure of the elderly population**[a]

	% of population 65 + aged	1980	1990	2000	2010	2020	2030	2040	2050
Australia	65-69	37.4	34.2	29.4	33.0	32.6	29.3	27.3	25.6
	70-79	45.2	46.6	47.9	42.1	46.0	45.4	44.0	42.4
	80 +	17.3	19.0	22.6	24.8	21.3	25.2	28.7	32.0
Austria	65-69	32.2	33.9	28.5	33.6	28.8	31.4	23.6	24.9
	70-79	50.2	42.3	50.3	42.3	46.3	43.8	48.8	40.2
	80 +	17.4	23.7	21.1	23.9	24.7	24.7	27.5	34.9
Belgium	65-69	31.7	29.1	32.9	31.5	32.8	31.9	27.2	27.6
	70-79	49.3	47.6	46.4	47.0	45.3	47.5	48.9	44.8
	80 +	18.9	23.2	20.5	21.3	21.8	20.5	23.9	27.6
Canada	65-69	36.0	34.3	30.2	31.9	32.3	28.8	23.5	24.6
	70-79	44.9	46.0	47.7	42.9	45.1	46.4	45.3	40.0
	80 +	18.9	19.5	22.0	25.1	22.5	24.6	31.2	33.1
Denmark	65-69	33.1	31.1	29.4	36.4	31.1	31.6	27.8	23.9
	70-79	47.3	46.7	47.2	42.8	50.8	45.3	48.6	46.8
	80 +	19.5	22.1	23.3	20.7	18.0	23.0	23.7	29.3
France	65-69	30.7	33.1	30.2	27.3	30.9	27.3	25.3	25.7
	70-79	48.8	39.9	47.9	44.0	43.5	45.4	44.3	41.4
	80 +	20.4	26.8	21.8	28.6	25.5	27.2	30.4	32.9
Germany	65-69	33.0	32.2	32.3	29.8	30.8	33.7	22.0	25.0
	70-79	50.2	43.2	46.3	49.1	44.2	45.1	51.7	38.8
	80 +	16.7	24.5	21.3	21.0	24.9	21.0	26.3	36.3
Greece	65-69	34.5	34.6	38.6	29.6	31.0	31.9	29.4	28.5
	70-79	47.9	47.2	47.1	50.3	45.9	46.1	48.3	46.6
	80 +	17.4	18.1	14.2	20.0	23.0	21.9	22.2	24.9
Iceland	65-69	31.8	32.3	31.8	32.1	36.9	33.8	28.3	28.3
	70-79	45.5	44.7	46.9	44.6	45.0	47.6	48.3	46.7
	80 +	22.5	22.9	21.1	23.1	17.9	18.4	23.3	25.0
Ireland	65-69	36.6	30.4	27.8	32.2	35.4	33.6	32.1	30.9
	70-79	46.3	49.2	46.0	43.0	45.5	47.2	46.6	46.6
	80 +	16.9	20.2	26.1	24.7	19.0	19.1	21.3	22.5
Italy	65-69	35.3	35.3	32.9	29.0	30.3	32.4	29.3	24.6
	70-79	48.0	44.4	49.6	48.4	46.1	44.6	48.0	47.3
	80 +	16.6	20.1	17.3	22.4	23.5	22.9	22.7	28.1
Japan	65-69	37.2	37.2	35.7	33.8	28.6	28.1	30.5	23.6
	70-79	47.5	44.4	47.8	46.9	49.6	44.5	44.7	47.6
	80 +	15.2	18.2	16.4	19.2	21.6	27.2	24.8	28.8
Luxembourg	65-69	34.4	30.8	30.8	28.7	30.8	28.6	24.4	27.0
	70-79	49.6	44.8	46.7	45.0	43.8	46.3	46.3	40.5
	80 +	15.9	24.2	22.4	26.2	25.3	25.0	29.3	32.4
Netherlands	65-69	33.2	32.4	31.0	34.5	33.0	30.7	25.6	24.7
	70-79	47.2	45.7	46.8	43.5	48.0	46.0	47.6	41.9
	80 +	19.5	21.8	22.0	21.9	18.8	23.1	26.7	33.3
New Zealand	65-69	36.6	34.1	30.4	35.5	34.9	32.8	28.8	26.3
	70-79	46.7	47.3	48.3	43.2	46.9	46.7	47.4	44.9
	80 +	16.5	18.5	21.1	21.2	18.0	20.4	23.9	28.9
Norway	65-69	33.1	30.6	25.6	33.2	32.0	29.7	27.3	24.8
	70-79	47.0	47.3	47.5	40.5	48.3	46.2	46.2	44.0
	80 +	19.8	22.0	26.7	26.1	19.6	24.0	26.4	31.2
Spain	65-69	34.7	33.7	32.3	28.5	30.3	31.8	29.6	24.9
	70-79	49.2	46.2	47.8	46.4	44.4	44.7	46.9	47.0
	80 +	16.0	20.0	19.8	25.0	25.2	23.4	23.5	28.2
Sweden	65-69	32.8	29.7	26.6	34.6	28.3	28.0	26.3	24.9
	70-79	48.0	47.0	46.6	41.2	49.8	43.6	46.2	44.0
	80 +	19.1	23.2	26.7	24.1	21.8	28.3	27.5	31.0
Switzerland	65-69	32.2	31.0	30.1	30.4	27.0	26.6	21.8	22.1
	70-79	48.9	44.5	45.4	43.2	45.9	42.5	44.8	38.9
	80 +	18.8	24.4	24.3	26.3	27.0	30.8	33.3	39.1

Table A.3.*(cont'd)*

	% of population 65 + aged	1980	1990	2000	2010	2020	2030	2040	2050
United Kingdom	65-69	33.9	32.5	29.9	33.0	31.0	32.7	25.4	27.4
	70-79	48.2	46.2	47.9	44.4	48.8	44.1	49.7	41.1
	80 +	17.8	21.2	22.1	22.5	20.1	23.0	24.8	31.5
United States	65-69	34.2	32.8	28.5	33.2	35.3	30.4	25.0	28.2
	70-79	45.4	46.3	47.9	42.3	45.2	48.3	46.1	40.9
	80 +	20.3	20.8	23.5	24.4	19.3	21.1	28.9	30.9

a) 1980 actual proportions; 1990 to 2050 projected proportions.
Source: See Table A.1.

Annex B

SOCIAL EXPENDITURE PROJECTIONS

SOURCES AND NOTES FOR TABLES IN ANNEX B

Expenditure totals for the various programmes in the base year, 1980, are taken from OECD, *Social Expenditure: 1960-1990*, Paris, 1984, Annex C and from OECD social expenditure data files. Per capita expenditure by age within the various programmes has been calculated in the case of Australia, Belgium and the Netherlands on the basis of the sources listed below. For the remaining nine countries, per capita expenditure on unemployment compensation has been calculated by averaging expenditure across the 15-64 age group and per capita expenditure on family benefits has been calculated on the basis of information on the age groups eligible for benefits. Per capita expenditure on education has been calculated on the basis of information on the share of public education expenditure allocated to each level of education and the age groups corresponding to the various levels. These data are contained in OECD, "Educational Costs, Expenditures and Financing: An Analysis of Trends", Paris (forthcoming). Per capita expenditure on pensions has been calculated by averaging pension expenditures (old age, survivors, invalidity) across the population aged 60 and over (55 in the case of Italy). Per capita expenditure by age on health has been calculated on the basis of the sources listed below. Where age-expenditure data are not available for 1980, data for the nearest available year have been used to derive age-expenditure coefficients, which have been applied to 1980 expenditure totals for each programme. Expenditure projections have been obtained by multiplying per capita expenditures by projected numbers in the corresponding age groups at five-year intervals.

Australia

The Impact of Population Changes on Social Expenditure: Projections from 1980-81 to 2021, Social Welfare Policy Secretariat, Canberra, 1984. Data refer to 1980-81.

Belgium

Incidence de l'Evolution Probable de la Population sur les Dépenses Sociales, Bureau du Plan, Brussels, 1985 (mimeo). Data refer to 1982.

Micheline Lambrecht, *Incidence de la Structure de la Population sur les Dépenses Sociales: Le cas de la Belgique de 1977 à 2000* (mimeo). Data refer to 1977.

Canada

Jac-André Boulet and Gilles Grenier, *Health Expenditures in Canada and the Impact of Demographic Changes on Future Government Health Insurance Program Expenditures*, Economic Council of Canada, Ottawa, 1978, Discussion Paper No. 123. Data refer to 1974.

Denmark

Data on health expenditure by age supplied by Ministry of Finance, Copenhagen. Data refer to 1983.

France

André Mizrahi et Arié Mizrahi, *Débours et Dépenses Medicales Selon l'Age et le Sexe: France 1970-1980*, Paris, Centre de Recherche, d'Etude et de Documentation en Economie de la Santé, 1985. Data refer to 1980-81.

Germany

Ralf Brennecke and Reinhard Hiersemenzel, *Gesundheitsleistungen 1981. Ergebnisse der Transferumfrage 1981*. J.W. Goethe - Universität Frankfurt und Universität Mannheim, 1984, Arbeitspapier Nr. 138. Data refer to 1975.

Italy

Indagine Statistica sulle Condizioni di Salute della Popolazione e sul Ricorso ai Servizi Sanitari nel Novembre 1980, Rome, ISTAT, 1982. Data refer to 1980.

Japan

Estimation of National Medical Care Expenses in Japan for Fiscal Year 1981 (April 1981 - March 1982), Statistics and Information Department, Ministry of Health and Welfare, Tokyo, 1984. Data refer to 1980.

Netherlands

Goudriaan, René *et al.*, *Collectieve uitgaven en demografische ontwikkeling, 1970-2030*, Social and Cultural Planning Bureau, Rijswijk, 1984. Data refer to 1981.

Sweden

Information on health expenditure by age supplied by Ministry of Health and Social Affairs, Stockholm. Data refer to 1983.

United Kingdom

The Government's Expenditure Plans 1982-83 to 1984-85, Vol. 2, HMSO, London, 1982. Data refer to England, 1979-80.

United States

Fischer, Charles R., "Differences by Age Groups in Health Care Spending", *Health Care Financing Review*, Spring 1980. Data refer to 1978.

Table B.1.   **The implications of demographic change for expenditure on the major social programmes, 1980 - 2040**

In millions of national currency

	1980	1985	1990	1995	2000	2005	2010	2015	2020	2025	2030	2035	2040
Australia													
Education	100	103	105	107	109	111	113	114	117	119	122	125	128
	7 692	7 910	8 058	8 240	8 379	8 572	8 696	8 803	8 971	9 170	9 396	9 633	9 871
Family benefits	100	101	101	105	107	108	109	110	113	116	120	123	126
	953	960	964	999	1 021	1 034	1 040	1 051	1 076	1 109	1 142	1 171	1 200
Health	100	111	122	132	143	152	162	172	185	202	217	229	240
	6 153	6 806	7 482	8 148	8 787	9 372	9 946	10 597	11 402	12 440	13 336	14 105	14 753
Unemployment	100	107	114	117	121	127	131	133	135	137	139	142	145
	996	1 071	1 132	1 166	1 206	1 260	1 300	1 326	1 346	1 362	1 384	1 411	1 440
Pensions	100	113	126	136	146	159	176	195	216	241	261	277	288
	7 111	8 067	8 943	9 675	10 395	11 298	12 486	13 891	15 381	17 124	18 587	19 686	20 467
Total[a]	100	108	116	123	130	137	146	155	166	179	190	200	207
	24 542	26 582	28 473	30 235	31 894	33 740	35 781	38 109	40 756	43 952	46 738	49 024	50 860
Belgium													
Education	100	95	89	85	84	82	78	75	72	71	71	72	71
	272 960	260 309	243 521	232 791	228 941	223 570	213 966	203 566	196 764	194 700	195 070	195 340	194 847
Family benefits	100	96	91	88	86	83	80	77	75	74	74	74	74
	90 200	86 557	82 477	79 721	77 736	75 035	71 773	69 012	67 485	67 050	67 029	66 957	66 835
Health	100	101	101	101	101	102	103	103	104	104	103	101	99
	173 402	174 799	175 163	175 574	175 614	176 218	177 812	179 286	180 208	180 218	178 714	175 569	171 330
Unemployment	100	102	103	101	98	98	99	99	98	94	90	86	84
	99 100	100 746	102 215	99 642	97 266	97 377	97 853	98 567	96 741	93 376	89 271	85 568	83 588
Pensions	100	104	103	103	104	106	112	118	124	131	135	136	136
	419 700	436 047	434 138	430 700	434 913	444 940	471 719	496 810	522 350	548 189	565 410	570 803	561 661
Total	100	100	98	97	96	96	98	99	101	103	104	104	102
	1 055 362	1 058 457	1 037 515	1 018 429	1 014 470	1 017 139	1 033 122	1 047 241	1 063 549	1 083 533	1 095 495	1 094 237	1 078 261
Canada													
Education	100	95	92	92	93	93	92	91	91	93	96	100	103
	18 251	17 427	16 726	16 746	16 975	16 999	16 835	16 579	16 604	17 002	17 598	18 231	18 842
Family benefits	100	96	95	97	98	96	94	94	96	100	103	107	110
	1 864	1 787	1 780	1 816	1 825	1 791	1 748	1 746	1 792	1 861	1 928	1 989	2 053
Health	100	109	119	129	139	148	159	170	182	195	206	214	218
	16 478	18 000	19 536	21 241	22 888	24 352	26 219	28 046	30 034	32 127	33 914	35 257	35 964
Unemployment	100	107	111	116	121	126	130	131	130	128	127	127	129
	7 140	7 612	7 935	8 248	8 607	8 997	9 265	9 336	9 286	9 152	9 045	9 069	9 193
Pensions	100	116	130	142	153	169	196	226	259	287	302	306	304
	13 577	15 753	17 638	19 289	20 774	22 933	26 638	30 719	35 158	38 977	40 999	41 512	41 325
Total	100	106	111	118	124	131	141	151	162	173	181	185	187
	57 310	60 579	63 615	67 340	71 068	75 072	80 705	86 427	92 874	99 119	103 484	106 058	107 377

[First country]

Education	100	95	88	80	74	69	67	63	60	58	57	58	58
	29 313	27 952	25 730	23 363	21 720	20 281	19 532	18 565	17 578	16 936	16 742	16 872	17 080
Family benefits	100	88	80	75	73	70	65	61	58	59	60	61	61
	4 714	4 168	3 769	3 513	3 417	3 281	3 061	2 855	2 753	2 774	2 844	2 880	2 863
Health	100	102	103	101	100	98	99	99	99	97	98	97	95
	21 648	22 163	22 199	21 952	21 550	21 263	21 324	21 535	21 336	21 081	21 217	21 087	20 632
Unemployment	100	103	103	104	103	101	97	93	88	84	78	73	70
	15 223	15 609	15 740	15 811	15 642	15 377	14 830	14 085	13 439	12 711	11 916	11 143	10 606
Pensions	100	104	102	99	99	105	114	118	120	123	128	128	124
	30 320	31 548	30 998	30 155	29 955	31 724	34 479	35 721	36 496	37 348	38 853	38 767	37 713
Total	100	100	97	94	91	91	92	92	91	90	90	90	88
	101 217	101 440	98 437	94 794	92 286	91 926	93 226	92 761	91 602	90 850	91 573	90 750	88 895

France

Education	100	97	93	91	90	88	84	81	79	78	79	80	80
	158 300	153 505	147 079	144 200	142 745	139 061	133 692	128 583	125 234	124 263	124 855	125 870	126 497
Family benefits	100	97	95	94	91	88	84	82	82	82	83	83	83
	73 641	71 527	69 749	69 403	67 324	64 582	62 093	60 539	60 173	60 552	61 065	61 337	61 296
Health	100	102	105	107	110	113	115	117	119	120	121	120	119
	169 898	174 016	177 790	182 276	187 351	192 292	195 832	199 404	202 438	204 585	205 553	204 702	202 576
Unemployment	100	105	107	108	109	111	112	110	107	105	102	99	97
	45 323	47 707	48 590	48 795	49 425	50 295	50 734	49 922	48 622	47 385	46 130	44 941	44 092
Pensions	100	109	115	120	122	128	140	152	161	169	175	176	172
	318 473	346 331	365 481	381 333	388 982	408 101	445 514	483 258	512 406	538 184	556 003	559 005	546 890
Total	100	104	106	108	109	112	116	120	124	127	130	130	128
	765 635	793 087	808 689	826 006	835 826	854 332	887 865	921 705	948 872	974 969	993 606	995 855	981 351

Germany

Education	100	87	75	70	70	68	63	58	54	53	54	54	53
	75 800	65 846	56 728	52 794	52 847	51 791	47 970	43 612	40 745	40 086	40 554	40 697	40 066
Family benefits	100	84	81	83	81	74	66	62	62	63	63	62	60
	16 930	14 225	13 645	14 027	13 632	12 459	11 181	10 479	10 454	10 667	10 685	10 447	10 191
Health	100	102	103	103	104	104	104	103	100	97	94	93	90
	96 722	98 297	99 513	99 594	100 208	100 798	100 730	99 678	96 943	93 440	90 906	89 710	86 906
Unemployment	100	105	104	101	98	95	92	89	84	78	71	66	63
	13 480	14 118	13 972	13 605	13 269	12 761	12 384	11 956	11 272	10 452	9 529	8 847	8 558
Pensions	100	104	107	112	122	126	126	128	131	138	141	136	126
	179 450	187 326	192 784	200 397	218 033	225 396	225 495	228 988	235 527	247 829	252 212	244 341	225 235
Total	100	99	98	99	104	105	104	103	103	105	106	103	97
	382 382	379 813	376 642	380 416	397 989	403 205	397 759	394 713	394 941	402 474	403 886	394 043	370 956

Table B.1. (cont'd)

	1980	1985	1990	1995	2000	2005	2010	2015	2020	2015	2030	2035	2040
Italy[b]													
Education	100	97	91	83	76	73	71	68	63	61	60	61	62
	19 022	18 534	17 229	15 709	14 435	13 866	13 515	12 851	12 075	11 530	11 402	11 588	11 823
Family benefits	100	91	83	78	75	73	69	64	62	62	63	64	64
	3 394	3 096	2 831	2 650	2 562	2 478	2 332	2 185	2 100	2 099	2 145	2 182	2 184
Health	100	103	105	107	109	112	114	115	115	115	114	111	108
	20 319	20 866	21 433	21 768	22 153	22 688	23 092	23 270	23 304	23 314	23 114	22 644	21 892
Unemployment	100	104	106	105	104	102	101	99	95	91	86	81	77
	1 589	1 659	1 685	1 676	1 650	1 623	1 609	1 565	1 516	1 451	1 366	1 290	1 227
Pensions	100	106	109	114	114	122	126	130	136	141	143	140	134
	40 093	42 314	43 801	45 525	45 887	48 893	50 495	52 050	54 477	56 361	57 384	56 267	53 618
Total	100	102	103	103	103	106	108	109	111	112	113	111	107
	84 417	86 468	86 979	87 327	86 687	89 548	91 044	91 921	93 472	94 755	95 411	93 970	90 744
Japan[b]													
Education	100	101	95	86	81	83	87	87	84	80	78	79	79
	11 742	11 851	11 125	10 093	9 564	9 762	10 164	10 227	9 852	9 393	9 193	9 228	9 247
Family benefits	100	95	87	81	82	85	86	84	90	78	78	78	77
	3 790	3 619	3 305	3 086	3 110	3 225	3 271	3 184	3 039	2 955	2 950	2 958	2 927
Health	100	109	117	127	135	141	145	149	151	148	144	145	146
	10 941	11 885	12 841	13 852	14 729	15 374	15 892	16 322	16 492	16 212	15 795	15 833	15 984
Unemployment	100	105	109	110	109	106	103	101	99	99	97	94	91
	954	1 005	1 044	1 050	1 036	1 011	982	959	948	943	926	898	869
Pensions	100	117	138	160	180	201	219	225	220	215	216	227	229
	10 601	12 359	14 626	16 912	19 105	21 321	23 189	23 841	23 335	22 827	22 940	24 109	24 283
Total	100	107	113	118	125	133	141	143	141	138	136	139	140
	38 028	40 719	42 941	44 993	47 544	50 693	53 499	54 533	53 667	52 329	51 803	53 026	53 310
Netherlands													
Education	100	96	91	89	86	84	82	76	74	74	73	72	70
	24 210	23 129	22 076	21 440	20 868	20 305	19 812	18 506	17 999	17 826	17 649	17 368	17 024
Family benefits	100	94	88	85	82	81	80	75	73	72	71	70	69
	6 970	6 537	6 131	5 898	5 727	5 628	5 552	5 201	5 065	4 995	4 955	4 899	4 825
Health	100	105	108	112	115	117	121	124	128	133	137	138	137
	21 761	22 775	23 548	24 334	25 022	25 533	26 293	27 034	27 773	29 019	29 726	30 007	29 773
Unemployment	100	106	109	110	111	112	111	108	104	99	94	90	87
	5 620	5 958	6 148	6 183	6 231	6 268	6 219	6 048	5 829	5 573	5 298	5 056	4 904
Pensions	100	107	114	121	127	133	140	149	154	160	163	163	160
	37 040	39 586	42 088	44 768	47 081	49 182	52 039	55 301	57 211	59 118	60 233	60 427	59 323
Total[a]	100	103	105	108	111	113	115	117	119	122	123	123	121
	107 421	110 603	113 154	116 161	118 769	120 874	123 946	126 099	127 957	130 953	132 324	132 134	130 101

Sweden

Education	100	96	91	88	87	86	85	83	82	83	82	83	83
	34 330	32 814	31 379	30 274	29 934	29 663	29 277	28 656	28 161	28 020	28 155	28 352	28 475
Family benefits	100	94	89	88	88	87	85	83	82	82	83	84	84
	8 368	7 857	7 446	7 323	7 328	7 305	7 150	6 953	6 862	6 896	6 980	7 029	7 032
Health	100	105	107	108	107	105	104	108	114	118	119	118	117
	46 074	48 584	49 479	49 642	49 260	48 273	47 973	49 830	52 489	54 555	54 608	54 174	54 011
Unemployment	100	101	102	102	103	103	101	98	97	95	93	90	89
	2 044	2 068	2 077	2 091	2 100	2 101	2 064	2 012	1 978	1 946	1 900	1 850	1 823
Pensions	100	105	104	101	98	103	111	117	121	124	126	126	123
	57 167	60 298	59 559	57 508	56 287	58 899	63 218	66 949	68 954	70 793	72 293	71 818	70 377
Total	100	102	101	99	98	99	101	104	107	110	111	110	109
	147 983	151 621	149 940	146 838	144 910	146 241	149 682	154 400	158 443	162 211	163 936	163 223	161 718

United Kingdom

Education	100	96	90	86	87	91	91	91	90	90	90	88	85
	12 718	12 250	11 468	10 969	11 110	11 515	11 557	11 559	11 481	11 456	11 389	11 152	10 786
Family benefits	100	93	90	94	97	96	95	95	96	96	93	89	86
	2 989	2 773	2 686	2 800	2 885	2 882	2 851	2 841	2 865	2 855	2 770	2 651	2 574
Health	100	103	103	103	104	103	104	106	108	114	117	119	121
	11 787	12 104	12 121	12 131	12 206	12 170	12 255	12 481	12 783	13 399	13 767	14 054	14 241
Unemployment	100	103	104	103	104	105	105	104	104	103	101	99	99
	2 127	2 200	2 205	2 187	2 204	2 225	2 238	2 221	2 208	2 188	2 148	2 115	2 111
Pensions	100	104	102	100	98	100	107	111	116	128	136	136	130
	15 095	15 683	15 416	15 113	14 852	15 157	16 084	16 687	17 562	19 338	20 557	20 552	19 637
Total	100	101	98	97	97	98	101	102	105	110	113	113	110
	44 716	45 009	43 897	43 201	43 257	43 949	44 984	45 790	46 899	49 236	50 631	50 524	49 349

United States

Education	100	95	94	95	98	99	98	97	97	99	100	101	102
	148 000	140 722	138 764	140 917	144 554	146 285	144 350	143 150	143 936	146 326	148 449	149 839	151 031
Family benefits	100	101	106	111	109	106	105	107	110	111	111	112	114
	12 409	12 551	13 116	13 764	13 539	13 168	13 046	13 287	13 609	13 777	13 828	13 915	14 124
Health	100	107	113	117	121	124	131	141	152	164	172	177	178
	105 426	113 209	119 146	123 769	127 274	131 221	138 169	148 420	160 751	173 228	181 808	187 024	187 685
Unemployment	100	105	109	112	118	123	126	127	126	124	123	124	126
	16 097	16 922	17 507	18 043	18 924	19 773	20 306	20 426	20 273	20 008	19 878	20 018	20 265
Pensions	100	100	114	116	119	128	144	165	188	205	213	217	215
	186 662	204 715	213 504	217 344	222 768	238 994	268 168	307 071	350 298	383 393	397 478	404 623	400 858
Total	100	104	107	110	112	117	125	135	147	157	162	165	165
	468 594	488 119	502 036	513 838	527 060	549 440	584 038	632 354	688 866	736 643	761 442	775 420	773 963

a) Totals do not correspond to the sum of programmes shown because other social expenditures are included in calculations.
b) Data for Italy and Japan are expressed in billions.
Source: OECD Secretariat estimates.

Table B.2. **The implications of demographic change for the distribution of social expenditure among the major programmes, 1980 - 2040**[a]

Percentages

	1980	1985	1990	1995	2000	2005	2010	2015	2020	2025	2030	2035	2040
Australia													
Education	31	30	28	27	26	25	24	23	22	21	20	20	19
Health	25	26	26	27	28	28	28	28	28	28	29	29	29
Pensions	29	30	31	32	33	33	35	36	38	39	40	40	40
Belgium													
Education	26	25	23	23	23	22	21	19	19	18	18	18	18
Health	16	17	17	17	17	17	17	17	17	17	16	16	16
Pensions	40	41	42	42	43	44	46	47	49	51	52	52	52
Canada													
Education	32	29	26	25	24	23	21	19	18	17	17	17	18
Health	29	30	31	32	32	32	32	32	32	32	33	33	33
Pensions	24	26	28	29	29	31	33	36	38	39	40	39	38
Denmark													
Education	29	28	26	25	24	22	21	20	19	19	18	19	19
Health	21	22	23	23	23	23	23	23	23	23	23	23	23
Pensions	30	31	31	32	32	35	37	39	40	41	42	43	42
France													
Education	21	19	18	17	17	16	15	14	13	13	13	13	13
Health	22	22	22	22	22	23	22	22	21	21	21	21	21
Pensions	42	44	45	46	47	48	50	52	54	55	56	56	56
Germany													
Education	20	17	15	14	13	13	12	11	10	10	10	10	11
Health	25	26	26	26	25	25	25	25	25	23	23	23	23
Pensions	47	49	51	53	55	56	57	58	60	62	62	62	61
Italy													
Education	23	21	20	18	17	15	15	14	13	12	12	12	13
Health	24	24	25	25	26	25	25	25	25	25	24	24	24
Pensions	47	49	50	52	53	55	55	57	58	59	60	60	59
Japan													
Education	31	29	26	22	20	19	19	19	18	18	18	17	17
Health	29	29	30	31	31	30	30	30	31	31	30	30	30
Pensions	28	30	34	38	40	42	43	44	43	44	44	45	46
Netherlands													
Education	23	21	20	18	18	17	16	15	14	14	13	13	13
Health	20	21	21	21	21	21	21	21	22	22	22	23	23
Pensions	34	36	37	39	40	41	42	44	45	45	46	46	46
Sweden													
Education	23	22	21	21	21	20	20	19	18	17	17	17	18
Health	31	32	33	34	34	33	32	32	33	34	33	33	33
Pensions	39	40	40	39	39	40	42	43	44	44	44	44	44
United Kingdom													
Education	28	27	26	25	26	26	26	25	24	23	22	22	22
Health	26	27	28	28	28	28	27	27	27	27	27	28	29
Pensions	34	35	35	35	34	34	36	36	37	39	41	41	40
United States													
Education	32	29	28	27	27	27	25	23	21	20	19	19	20
Health	22	23	24	24	24	24	24	23	23	24	24	24	24
Pensions	40	42	43	42	42	43	46	49	51	52	52	52	52

a) Expenditure is expressed as a percentage of the totals shown in Table B.1.
Source: OECD Secretariat estimates.

WHERE TO OBTAIN OECD PUBLICATIONS
OÙ OBTENIR LES PUBLICATIONS DE L'OCDE

ARGENTINA - ARGENTINE
Carlos Hirsch S.R.L.,
Florida 165, 4º Piso,
(Galeria Guemes) 1333 Buenos Aires
Tel. 33.1787.2391 y 30.7122

AUSTRALIA - AUSTRALIE
D.A. Book (Aust.) Pty. Ltd.
11-13 Station Street (P.O. Box 163)
Mitcham, Vic. 3132   Tel. (03) 873 4411

AUSTRIA - AUTRICHE
OECD Publications and Information Centre,
4 Simrockstrasse,
5300 Bonn (Germany)   Tel. (0228) 21.60.45
Gerold & Co., Graben 31, Wien 1 Tel. 52.22.35

BELGIUM - BELGIQUE
Jean de Lannoy,
Avenue du Roi 202
B-1060 Bruxelles   Tel. (02) 538.51.69

CANADA
Renouf Publishing Company Ltd/
Éditions Renouf Ltée,
1294 Algoma Road, Ottawa, Ont. K1B 3W8
Tel: (613) 741-4333
Toll Free/Sans Frais:
Ontario, Quebec, Maritimes:
1-800-267-1805
Western Canada, Newfoundland:
1-800-267-1826
Stores/Magasins:
61 rue Sparks St., Ottawa, Ont. K1P 5A6
Tel: (613) 238-8985
211 rue Yonge St., Toronto, Ont. M5B 1M4
Tel: (416) 363-3171
Federal Publications Inc.,
301-303 King St. W.,
Toronto, Ont. M5V 1J5
Tel. (416)581-1552
Les Éditions la Liberté inc.,
3020 Chemin Sainte-Foy,
Sainte-Foy, P.Q. G1X 3V6,
Tel. (418)658-3763

DENMARK - DANEMARK
Munksgaard Export and Subscription Service
35, Nørre Søgade, DK-1370 København K
Tel. +45.1.12.85.70

FINLAND - FINLANDE
Akateeminen Kirjakauppa,
Keskuskatu 1, 00100 Helsinki 10   Tel. 0.12141

FRANCE
OCDE/OECD
Mail Orders/Commandes par correspondance :
2, rue André-Pascal,
75775 Paris Cedex 16
Tel. (1) 45.24.82.00
Bookshop/Librairie : 33, rue Octave-Feuillet
75016 Paris
Tel. (1) 45.24.81.67 or/ou (1) 45.24.81.81
Librairie de l'Université,
12a, rue Nazareth,
13602 Aix-en-Provence   Tel. 42.26.18.08

GERMANY - ALLEMAGNE
OECD Publications and Information Centre,
4 Simrockstrasse,
5300 Bonn   Tel. (0228) 21.60.45

GREECE - GRÈCE
Librairie Kauffmann,
28, rue du Stade, 105 64 Athens Tel. 322.21.60

HONG KONG
Government Information Services,
Publications (Sales) Office,
Information Services Department
No. 1, Battery Path, Central

ICELAND - ISLANDE
Snæbjörn Jónsson & Co., h.f.,
Hafnarstræti 4 & 9,
P.O.B. 1131 – Reykjavik
Tel. 13133/14281/11936

INDIA - INDE
Oxford Book and Stationery Co.,
Scindia House, New Delhi 110001
Tel. 331.5896/5308
17 Park St., Calcutta 700016   Tel. 240832

INDONESIA - INDONÉSIE
Pdii-Lipi, P.O. Box 3065/JKT.Jakarta
Tel. 583467

IRELAND - IRLANDE
TDC Publishers - Library Suppliers,
12 North Frederick Street, Dublin 1
Tel. 744835-749677

ITALY - ITALIE
Libreria Commissionaria Sansoni,
Via Lamarmora 45, 50121 Firenze
Tel. 579751/584468
Via Bartolini 29, 20155 Milano   Tel. 365083
La diffusione delle pubblicazioni OCSE viene
assicurata dalle principali librerie ed anche da :
Editrice e Libreria Herder,
Piazza Montecitorio 120, 00186 Roma
Tel. 6794628
Libreria Hœpli,
Via Hœpli 5, 20121 Milano   Tel. 865446
Libreria Scientifica
Dott. Lucio de Biasio "Aeiou"
Via Meravigli 16, 20123 Milano   Tel. 807679

JAPAN - JAPON
OECD Publications and Information Centre,
Landic Akasaka Bldg., 2-3-4 Akasaka,
Minato-ku, Tokyo 107   Tel. 586.2016

KOREA - CORÉE
Kyobo Book Centre Co. Ltd.
P.O.Box: Kwang Hwa Moon 1658,
Seoul   Tel. (REP) 730.78.91

LEBANON - LIBAN
Documenta Scientifica/Redico,
Edison Building, Bliss St.,
P.O.B. 5641, Beirut   Tel. 354429-344425

**MALAYSIA/SINGAPORE -
MALAISIE/SINGAPOUR**
University of Malaya Co-operative Bookshop
Ltd.,
7 Lrg 51A/227A, Petaling Jaya
Malaysia   Tel. 7565000/7565425
Information Publications Pte Ltd
Pei-Fu Industrial Building,
24 New Industrial Road No. 02-06
Singapore 1953   Tel. 2831786, 2831798

NETHERLANDS - PAYS-BAS
SDU Uitgeverij
Christoffel Plantijnstraat 2
Postbus 20014
2500 EA's-Gravenhage   Tel. 070-789911
Voor bestellingen: Tel. 070-789880

NEW ZEALAND - NOUVELLE-ZÉLANDE
Government Printing Office Bookshops:
Auckland: Retail Bookshop, 25 Rutland Stseet,
Mail Orders, 85 Beach Road
Private Bag C.P.O.
Hamilton: Retail: Ward Street,
Mail Orders, P.O. Box 857
Wellington: Retail, Mulgrave Street, (Head
Office)
Cubacade World Trade Centre,
Mail Orders, Private Bag
Christchurch: Retail, 159 Hereford Street,
Mail Orders, Private Bag
Dunedin: Retail, Princes Street,
Mail Orders, P.O. Box 1104

NORWAY - NORVÈGE
Tanum-Karl Johan
Karl Johans gate 43, Oslo 1
PB 1177 Sentrum, 0107 Oslo 1Tel. (02) 42.93.10

PAKISTAN
Mirza Book Agency
65 Shahrah Quaid-E-Azam, Lahore 3 Tel. 66839

PHILIPPINES
I.J. Sagun Enterprises, Inc.
P.O. Box 4322 CPO Manila
Tel. 695-1946, 922-9495

PORTUGAL
Livraria Portugal,
Rua do Carmo 70-74,
1117 Lisboa Codex   Tel. 360582/3

**SINGAPORE/MALAYSIA -
SINGAPOUR/MALAISIE**
See "Malaysia/Singapor". Voir
« Malaisie/Singapour »

SPAIN - ESPAGNE
Mundi-Prensa Libros, S.A.,
Castelló 37, Apartado 1223, Madrid-28001
Tel. 431.33.99
Libreria Bosch, Ronda Universidad 11,
Barcelona 7   Tel. 317.53.08/317.53.58

SWEDEN - SUÈDE
AB CE Fritzes Kungl. Hovbokhandel,
Box 16356, S 103 27 STH,
Regeringsgatan 12,
DS Stockholm   Tel. (08) 23.89.00
Subscription Agency/Abonnements:
Wennergren-Williams AB,
Box 30004, S104 25 Stockholm Tel. (08)54.12.00

SWITZERLAND - SUISSE
OECD Publications and Information Centre,
4 Simrockstrasse,
5300 Bonn (Germany)   Tel. (0228) 21.60.45
Librairie Payot,
6 rue Grenus, 1211 Genève 11
Tel. (022) 31.89.50
United Nations Bookshop/Librairie des Nations-
Unies
Palais des Nations,
1211 – Geneva 10
Tel. 022-34-60-11 (ext. 48 72)

TAIWAN - FORMOSE
Good Faith Worldwide Int'l Co., Ltd.
9th floor, No. 118, Sec.2
Chung Hsiao E. Road
Taipei   Tel. 391.7396/391.7397

THAILAND - THAILANDE
Suksit Siam Co., Ltd., 1715 Rama IV Rd.,
Samyam Bangkok 5   Tel. 2511630
INDEX Book Promotion & Service Ltd.
59/6 Soi Lang Suan, Ploenchit Road
Patjumamwan, Bangkok 10500
Tel. 250-1919, 252-1066

TURKEY - TURQUIE
Kültur Yayinlari Is-Türk Ltd. Sti.
Atatürk Bulvari No: 191/Kat. 21
Kavaklidere/Ankara   Tel. 25.07.60
Dolmabahce Cad. No: 29
Besiktas/Istanbul   Tel. 160.71.88

UNITED KINGDOM - ROYAUME-UNI
H.M. Stationery Office,
Postal orders only: (01)211-5656
P.O.B. 276, London SW8 5DT
Telephone orders: (01) 622.3316, or
Personal callers:
49 High Holborn, London WC1V 6HB
Branches at: Belfast, Birmingham,
Bristol, Edinburgh, Manchester

UNITED STATES - ÉTATS-UNIS
OECD Publications and Information Centre,
2001 L Street, N.W., Suite 700,
Washington, D.C. 20036 - 4095
Tel. (202) 785.6323

VENEZUELA
Libreria del Este,
Avda F. Miranda 52, Aptdo. 60337,
Edificio Galipan, Caracas 106
Tel. 951.17.05/951.23.07/951.12.97

YUGOSLAVIA - YOUGOSLAVIE
Jugoslovenska Knjiga, Knez Mihajlova 2,
P.O.B. 36, Beograd   Tel. 621.992

Orders and inquiries from countries where
Distributors have not yet been appointed should be
sent to:
OECD, Publications Service, 2, rue André-Pascal,
75775 PARIS CEDEX 16.

Les commandes provenant de pays où l'OCDE n'a
pas encore désigné de distributeur doivent être
adressées à :
OCDE, Service des Publications. 2, rue André-
Pascal, 75775 PARIS CEDEX 16.

71784-05-1988

OECD PUBLICATIONS, 2, rue André-Pascal, 75775 PARIS CEDEX 16 - N° 44359 1988
PRINTED IN FRANCE
(81 88 02 1) ISBN 92-64-13113-2